WARREN HASTINGS.

THOMAS BABINGTON MACAULAY

WARREN HASTINGS

EDITED BY

ARTHUR D. INNES, M.A.

AUTHOR OF

"BRITAIN AND HER RIVALS IN THE EIGHTEENTH CENTURY"

CAMBRIDGE:
AT THE UNIVERSITY PRESS

1916

CAMBRIDGE UNIVERSITY PRESS
Cambridge, New York, Melbourne, Madrid, Cape Town,
Singapore, São Paulo, Delhi, Mexico City

Cambridge University Press
The Edinburgh Building, Cambridge CB2 8RU, UK

Published in the United States of America by Cambridge University Press, New York

www.cambridge.org
Information on this title: www.cambridge.org/9781107621763

First edition 1896
First published 1896
Reprinted 1898, 1901, 1904, 1907, 1913, 1916
First paperback edition 2013

A catalogue record for this publication is available from the British Library

ISBN 978-1-107-62176-3 Paperback

CONTENTS.

		PAGES
INTRODUCTION		vii—xxxv
I.	Macaulay and the Essay	vii—xi
II.	The Establishing of the British in India .	xii—xxxiv
III.	Of Indian Terms	xxxiv, xxxv
WARREN HASTINGS		1—142
NOTES		143—176
INDEX		177—179

MAPS :

INDIA, showing the principal States
The Carnatic   } . . *at end*

Northern and Central India . . . . "

INTRODUCTION.

I. MACAULAY; AND THE ESSAY.

§ 1. *Biographical.*

THOMAS BABINGTON MACAULAY was born on October 25th, 1800. His father, Zachary Macaulay, was sprung of a Scotch Presbyterian stock; and was in his day well known as a philanthropist, an active worker for the abolition of the slave-trade, and a friend of many notable Whigs. Young Thomas was brought up in the eminently respectable and religious society for which Clapham in the days of Hannah More was famous. From his earliest youth he was an omnivorous reader, and being endowed with an amazing memory he accumulated vast quantities of knowledge with surprising ease. As a boy, his precocity was nothing short of portentous.

In due course he went to Cambridge, where his progress was highly successful; and commenced his literary career immediately after taking his degree. In 1825 appeared his Essay on Milton, in the *Edinburgh Review*, at that time perhaps the leading literary periodical. Politics however claimed him. He was an able and incisive speaker, and had won much applause in debate at Cambridge; and in 1830 he entered Parliament through the influence of the Hollands, on the Whig side, as member for Lord Lansdowne's pocket-borough of Calne. He took an active part in the Reform debates, and gained fresh reputation when he sat in the new Parliament for Leeds after the great Reform Bill had been carried, in 1832. He was placed on the Indian Board of Control, and in 1833 went out to Calcutta as a Member of Council. Here he remained for five years, till 1838, and in this time devoted his personal experience to confirming all his previously formed ideas as to the history

and government of India. On his return to England he resumed his parliamentary career, and frequently held office, but
never attained fully to the very first rank as a parliamentarian.
Throughout these years he continued a constant and valuable
contributor to the *Edinburgh*, wherein one after another of his
Essays appeared. He was raised to the peerage in 1857, and
died in 1859.

§ 2. *Critical.*

Whatever judgment may be ultimately passed by posterity
on Macaulay as an historian, one great achievement may be
claimed for him, that he made history popular. His own
history and his biographical and historical essays have found
their way, and still find their way, where no predecessor of his
could get a hearing; and wherever Macaulay has dealt with
any subject, his successors have been more or less compelled
to write with the deliberate intention of either removing or
confirming popular impressions for which he is responsible.

This means at least that Macaulay's literary excellence
is of a very high order. It means that he can excite interest
where others have failed to do so; and that he makes a lasting
impression which, however erroneous, is singularly difficult to
eradicate.

This effect is due in the first place to his having formed a
style which is peculiarly lucid and coherent; and while never
overloaded with ornament is still adorned with a wealth of apt
illustration which keeps the intellect pleasantly stimulated.

In the second place, Macaulay always writes with an air of
conviction and reasonableness combined which is in itself
convincing. The mere air of conviction does not convince; it
may merely arouse antagonism. It is possible to be so reasonable that conviction is left quivering in the balance. Conviction
is conveyed by the conjunction. Now Macaulay gives the impression that no one of his statements or opinions has caused
him a moment's hesitation, while there are always sufficient facts
and authorities in his favour to make them plausible.

These qualities of style are combined with a mental

characteristic which adds an immense persuasiveness. His point of view is that which is also natural to the average reader : his methods of thought are the same. He lives in the *via media*. He approves of sobriety and order. He dislikes eccentricities. He mistrusts ideals and enthusiasms which do not appeal to him at sight; he does not feel that they demand careful examination, that there may be some motive in them worth penetrating after; he regards them in fact as a kind of craze. Now this is precisely the attitude of the average Englishman towards any political question in which he has no disturbing purely personal interest. Consequently the view of any particular event or character which commends itself to Macaulay is *primâ facie* the view likely to commend itself to the average Englishman.

But style and mental attitude in combination would not have sufficed to make Macaulay's position so strong, without the immense industry and the prodigious memory which enabled him to accumulate and to assort his facts. The facts as he presents them may rest upon insufficient evidence, may be coloured by prejudice, may be associated in a wholly misleading manner; but at the worst they are gathered from sources in which Macaulay believed, they have authority however untrustworthy, and as a rule, when stripped of rhetorical setting, the *bare* facts have to be admitted. Macaulay's opinions and inferences may be challenged to any extent; but to convict him of mis-stating a date, a name, or a place is anything but an easy task.

Such broadly are the reasons why Macaulay has secured among the historians of England this unique position; that in the main he has made his opinions the opinions of the average man. We have now to examine those defects in his mental equipment which deprive him of the right to be placed actually in the first rank; which make it imperative for the serious student to revise with the utmost care the impressions produced on him whether by the History or by the Essays.

We have already dwelt upon the *average* character of his sympathies. This enables him not only to keep in touch with the average reader, but also to form a strikingly accurate judgment of average men and average movements; intelligent men actuated by commonplace motives; movements excited by commonplace desires. Both men and movements are often important enough. Somers and Walpole, the glorious Revolution and the 1832 Reform Bill, are excellent examples. These are subjects in dealing with which Macaulay was thoroughly in his element. But the very quality which enabled him to deal with these subjects with thorough understanding made him incompetent to treat adequately of greater men and greater causes. To him, the Cavaliers are little more than a crew of roystering swash-bucklers fighting for their own predominance: the Puritans, a collection of narrow-minded zealots. His sympathies are exclusively with the pure Parliamentarians who objected to being taxed against their will. To him, Cromwell is the man who used the prostration of the nation to place himself in the position of dictator—not the leader who raised his country, from the position of a third-rate power to which the incompetence of the Stuarts and the anarchy of civil war had reduced it, to the position of the arbiter of Europe. Chatham is a great orator, and a great war minister on the whole, but an impracticable politician. Yet Chatham found the country in a state of grovelling panic at the idea of a French war; and in four years he had swept every rival fleet off the seas and annihilated, for good and all, all European rivalry in India and in America, besides striking the first blow at the oligarchy which forty years of Whig supremacy had built up.

That fancy then which plays freely among superficial and accidental ideas Macaulay had in abundance, and to it he owes in great part his power of picturesque description: but in the penetrating sympathetic imagination which gives a grip of fundamental moving ideas he was deficient. And this brings us to another aspect of his imaginative deficiency. It appears as though the range of his intellectual vision had become finally fixed when he was little more than a boy. No amount of experience altered him. As he had seen things when he was five-and-twenty, so he saw them when he was five-and-forty.

The "Clive" might just as well have been written before he went to India as afterwards. No fresh ideas seem to touch him. The workmanship of his writing advances; his wealth of illustration accumulates; but there is hardly any discoverable advance in critical penetration. The essay on Milton is a brilliant Prize Essay; that on Warren Hastings is a glorified Prize Essay. The rhetorical art is greater in the later essay than in the earlier one; but the critical insight is of precisely the same order.

It is in these limitations that Macaulay's vital defect is to be found. Yet his worst fault is commonly held to be his want of impartiality. Still, paradoxical as it may sound, it is not altogether a fault for the historian to play the part of an advocate rather than a judge, provided that he is honest. The speeches of counsel are as necessary to the proper hearing of a case as the judge's summing up; it is the business of the jury to discount the rhetoric. Macaulay is openly and palpably an advocate. He is a Whig, with certain political doctrines, so to speak, in his blood. Anyone with a policy which did not square with those doctrines is suspect: if there is a doubt he does not get the benefit of it. Also the historian was personally devoted to the Holland connexion, and all transactions associated with the name of Fox are coloured by the fact. His Evangelical up-bringing gave him a bias against all High Church-and-State doctrine, which colours all his views on ecclesiastical matters. And out of these several formative influences arose what can only be called personal animosities against particular individuals. But the bias is always open and palpable. That it is a fault is undeniable; but from being so manifest it is less dangerous than the unconscious defect already named: and it leads to misrepresentation chiefly of individuals, while the other leads to misrepresentation of principles.

This Essay is a review, written three years after Macaulay's return from India, of Gleig's Memoir of Warren Hastings. It bears throughout the marks of exceedingly strong prepossessions, which not only led Macaulay into misunderstanding the motives of Hastings but beguiled him into unusually frequent mis-representations of fact.

II. THE ESTABLISHING OF THE BRITISH IN INDIA.

§ 1. *The Founding of the British Power in India.*

The history of the Indian career of Warren Hastings is the history of the successful struggle to maintain and to consolidate the position of the East India Company as a leading territorial Power; a position which had been acquired and established between the years 1744 and 1767 mainly by the genius of Robert Clive. To understand the task which Hastings had to perform, it is necessary to appreciate the condition of the Native Powers with whom he had to deal, and the course of that contest in which first the Frenchman Dupleix, and then the Englishman Clive, played the leading parts.

Through many centuries India was a tempting bait for a succession of conquerors who swept down through the passes of the Himalayas, and set up in various districts one foreign dynasty after another. In the sixteenth century the great Tartar dynasty of the Moguls was established ; and between the reigns of Baber and Aurungzebe who died in 1707 the sway of the great Mahommedan Power was spread over two-thirds of the peninsula. But Aurungzebe's successors were incapable ; the viceroys appointed to administer the great provinces of the unwieldy empire established themselves as practically independent monarchs : in the Punjab the Hindoo Sikhs were forming an independent confederacy : Rajputana, never fully subdued, threw off the yoke : and the Mahrattas overran central India.

In 1740 then—setting aside the Punjab and Rajputana, which do not enter into the conflict—the Mogul reigning at Delhi in the upper provinces of the Ganges was the nominal sovereign of the states on the Ganges basin ; i.e. of the districts about Delhi, of Oude, of Behar, and Bengal ; of the coast province of Orissa ; and, farther south, of the Deccan and the Carnatic. But in effect, the Nawab-Vizier of Oude, the Nawab of Bengal who held also Behar and Orissa, and the Nizam of the Deccan (or of Hyderabad) were independent princes; while the Nawab of the Carnatic was subordinate to the Nizam. In all these cases a population mainly Hindoo was ruled over by a Mussulman court and Mussulman soldiery; central India was overrun by the hordes of the Hindoo Mahrattas; and Mysore was shortly to become formidable under the low-born but very able Mahommedan adventurer, Hyder Ali.

Two great mercantile associations, the French and English East India Companies, had been granted the monopoly of the Indian trade by their respective Governments. The object of both Companies was trade; the idea of acquiring territory or political influence had not presented itself to either as being within the range of practical politics. They merely held trading stations or factories as tenants of the native viceroys; fortified and garrisoned only with a view to that amount of protection required by settlements in a country where the Government was unstable. The English had three principal settlements, at Calcutta, Madras, and Bombay; the French two, at Chandernagore near Calcutta, and at Pondicherry near Madras. The settlements in the Carnatic at this time were the most important.

In 1740 Dupleix was appointed governor of Pondicherry. The break-up of the Empire, and jealousy of British rivalry, suggested to this very able man the idea that by obtaining influence at the Native courts he could get rid of the British altogether. When war was declared between France and Great Britain the rival companies in the Carnatic attacked each other. The first phase of the war was brought to a close by the Peace of Aix-la-Chapelle: and during this time the great lesson had been learned that a small body of European troops, or of native troops trained and officered by Europeans, were more than a match for ten times their number of the miscellaneous levies which Oriental princes could bring into the field. In the struggle with the British, the advantage so far had been with the French, though Dupleix's triumphs were in a great degree neutralised by British successes on the other side of the globe; and he was obliged to restore Madras, which he had captured, in exchange for Louisburg on the St Lawrence, which the British had taken. But the struggle now assumed a broader aspect. The succession to the Nizamship was in dispute, and the title of the Nawab of the Carnatic was challenged. Dupleix saw that if he sided with one pair of the candidates, and helped to establish them respectively as Nizam and Nawab, he would secure paramount influence at court. The British gave their support to the opposing candidates. Dupleix's success at first was complete ; but the scale was turned by the brilliant military achievements of Clive ; and when Dupleix was recalled in 1754 the British candidate was Nawab of the Carnatic.

In 1756 war again broke out between France and England. The struggle was renewed in the Carnatic ; and this time the issue was decisive. The French met with an overwhelming reverse at the hands of Eyre Coote at Wandewash; the immense naval predominance of Great Britain made any sort of recuperation impossible ; and the Peace of Paris in 1763 left France with no military foothold, and no territory ; while the English were recognised as a military Power, and the Nawab of the Carnatic was their puppet.

It had been to some extent a question whether French or English were to attain political power in India. That question was settled by the struggle in the Carnatic, and its final issue was largely due to the fact that the French were cut off from assistance from Europe by the British naval superiority. We now enter upon the contest between the British and the Native dynasties.

Before the last phase of the struggle with the French began, the Nawab of Bengal had challenged the British to attack him by the outrage known as "the Black Hole of Calcutta." The result of this outrage was that Clive was despatched to Bengal to demand reparation. A conspiracy was set on foot by malcontents round the Nawab ; the British actively fomented the intrigue ; a great battle was fought at Plassey, Surajah Dowlah was overthrown, Meer Jaffier was set up as Nawab in his place, and Meer Jaffier found himself completely

in the hands of the British. The Company were masters
of Bengal, although at first they refused to accept the responsi-
bilities of sovereignty while enjoying to the full every advantage
of complete dominion.

A brief period of grave misrule followed Clive's departure
for England; a time during which the British in Bengal made
use of their position to extort from the Nawab exemptions from
taxation which drove him to extremities for means of supplying
his treasury; to extract gifts from his subordinates; and generally
to indulge in the gravest tyranny. Meer Jaffier was turned out
to make room for Meer Cossim; and Meer Cossim, resisting the
tyranny, had to take flight after perpetrating the massacre
of Patna. Bengal was threatened by the Vizier of Oude, who
was accompanied by Shah Alum, the heir to the throne of Delhi.
The danger was dispelled by Sir Hector Munro's great victory
of Buxar, a few days after Clive reappeared at Calcutta. Clive
faced the situation with splendid ability and courage. He
made a treaty with the Oude Vizier in which the principle
of British policy was laid down—the consolidation of Oude as
a buffer state covering Bengal from Mahratta or Afghan
aggression. He reorganised the administration, formally accepting for the Company the Diwanee, i.e. the control of the
financial affairs of the province; thus in effect making it the
responsible ruler, since all military control was already in
its hands: and he removed the standing temptation to misconduct and extortion, by at once forbidding all private trading
by the Company's servants, all receiving of presents, and at the
same time appropriating the salt-tax to their benefit so as
to provide them with adequate salaries: with these achievements,
Clive terminated his Indian career, returning finally to England
in 1767.

§ 2. *Between Clive and Warren Hastings.*

Thus the state of affairs in India, when Hastings in 1772
became the prime controller of British policy as Governor
of Bengal, may be clearly grasped.

The British were now the only European Power capable of wielding direct political influence ; and they were fully recognised as being from a military point of view at least a match for any of the great native states. As yet, however, the three presidencies of Bengal, Madras, and Bombay were independent of each other, and under no general control nearer than that exercised by the Board of Directors of the East India Company in London. Bombay had hitherto remained a mercantile settlement not mixing in politics. In Madras the Company had made no territorial acquisitions, except in the nature of military stations ; they had assumed none of the functions of Government, although the Nawab of the Carnatic was practically at their orders. In Bengal the state of affairs was more complex.

Here the Company were virtual rulers of the whole province, from the borders of Oude to the Ganges Delta. The administration of the revenue, of military affairs, and of foreign affairs was formally in their hands. But nominally there was still a Nawab of Bengal, whose officers they were ; much of the administration was in the hands of natives ; and roughly speaking it might almost be said that the Company could act as sovereign when it chose, and still repudiate responsibility when convenient ; the Mogul at Delhi being still nominally sovereign.

In each of the presidencies, government was in the hands of a Governor and Council : subject to orders from the Court of Directors at home, whose decisions again were liable to be upset by the Court of Proprietors (i.e. the general body of large shareholders) ; while Parliament might at any time insist on interfering.

Turning to the native states, we find in the south the kingdom of Mysore now developed into a formidable military power by Hyder Ali. The Nizam of Hyderabad was still a considerable potentate, whose position however was rendered uneasy by fear of three possible foes—the British, Hyder Ali, and the Mahrattas. Right across central India, from the Malabar coast and Guzerat on the west to Orissa on the east the great confederacy of the Mahrattas had spread their sway,

plundering subject populations at will and threatening the
Nizam on the south, Delhi and Oude on the north. They had
not set about constructing an empire. They were a loose
association of fighting Hindoo tribes, under five chiefs. Of
these, the recognised head was the Peshwa at Poona; the other
four were the Gaikwar or Guicowar of Baroda, Scindia, Holkar,
and the Bhonsla at Nagpore. The great wave of Mahratta
aggression had been arrested in 1761 by the Afghan Ahmed
Shah the Abdallee at the great battle of Paniput: but the
Afghan had retired and the Mahrattas again advanced. The
districts about Delhi were virtually in their power; they were
alternately threatening and intriguing with the Rohillas in
Rohilcund on the western frontier of Oude; they had tried to
wedge themselves into Oude by procuring Allahabad and Cora
from Shah Alum, to whom the British had assigned those
districts with the express intention that they should form a
barrier between Oude and the Mahrattas. This attempt
however was foiled by the British, who reoccupied the territory
themselves: subsequently making it over to the Nawab-Vizier
for a large sum of money. Rohilcund still lay between the
Mahrattas and Oude on the west: a territory in which it
is estimated that some forty thousand Rohillas, Mahommedan
Afghans and good soldiers, ruled over about a million Hindoos.
Oude itself, with its Mussulman Nawab, it was the policy
of Clive and of Hastings after him to establish as a state strong
enough to resist attacks by the Mahrattas or coming from
the north-west; a state which should be nominally independent, but effectively for military purposes at the command of
the British.

The leading facts to be grasped then are: the Mahrattas
were the one great confederacy which might be welded into
a dominating power; and their territories lay so that none
of the three British presidencies could send troops to another
overland without marching right through Mahratta country:
and at the same time, the Mahrattas reached close enough
to each of the three presidencies to be a source of danger
for any one of them. Hyder Ali, the Nizam, and the Mahrattas,

were all jealous of each other, but all three were still more
jealous of the British ; and the British at Madras had
succeeded in offending all three by entering upon engagements
which were mutually destructive.

§ 3. *The Mahrattas, Hyder Ali, and France.*

Although Macaulay speaks of Warren Hastings as revolving
great designs of conquest, the facts are in favour of a quite
different view of his settled policy.   There is little question that
his aim was the same which Clive had clearly pointed out
before his final departure from India.   He purposed not to
extend British dominion, not to challenge Native Powers, but
to consolidate administration, to settle government on a sound
financial basis, and to secure the frontiers of the territory
already acquired.   Before passing to the history of Bengal
under Hastings—to those aspects of Indian affairs in which
Hastings is most directly implicated, and on which the biographer must necessarily dwell at greater length—we will
briefly review those events outside Bengal which greatly com-
plicated the Governor-General's task, and but for the energetic if
sometimes unscrupulous manner in which he dealt with them
might in the end have cost us the Indian Empire.

The Peshwa at Poona, nominal head of the Mahrattas, was
an infant ; and the government was in the hands of a council of
regency.   But there was a claimant of the Peshwa's office,
Ragonath Rao, commonly known as Ragoba.   Ragoba appealed
to the British at Bombay to support his claim : which Hornby,
the governor, decided to do, moved no doubt by a feeling that
it was time for Bombay to have a turn in the game of native
politics.   The stations of Salsette and Bassein were to be the
reward of British aid.   It was about this time that Hastings
was appointed Governor-General (1774) and he at once exerted
his authority to stop the action of Bombay : but his instructions
were too late.   Hornby had acted, and met with a serious
reverse.   Foolish as it had been to wilfully challenge the
Mahrattas, it was now evident that it would be disastrous to

withdraw until British superiority had been reasserted. It became imperative therefore for Hastings to carry on military operations energetically; a second disaster befel the Bombay troops before the succours came from Bengal. Then indeed the British leaders Goddard, Popham, and Bruce, made it abundantly clear to the Mahratta chiefs that the blunderers of Bombay were not to be regarded as showing the measure of British capacity. But the recovery of lost *prestige* is much more difficult than the maintenance of *prestige* already won; and though in the issue, by 1781, some real ground had been gained, it was at great cost.

Before the Mahratta affair was terminated the Madras council had succeeded in provoking another war, this time with Mysore. They had succeeded in setting the Nizam against themselves by not helping him in his last quarrel with Hyder Ali. The Mahrattas were already engaged in war with the British. To irritate Hyder Ali at this point was to provoke him when his chances of a successful attack were at their best.

Now England was at this time at war with her American colonies, and in 1778 the French intervened in that war: followed in 1779 by Spain. There was a vital difference between the situation in this war and that of 1756–1763—in the former war, France had had her energies diverted from the naval contest with England by her share in the continental war against Frederick of Prussia; and Spain had not joined in till the French fleet was already crushed. Now, however, France and Spain came in fresh and almost together, while England, standing entirely alone, had a part of her energies drawn off by the struggle against her own colonies. Hence it was as much as the British fleet could do to hold its own.

This had an important bearing on Indian affairs. France had no foothold on the peninsula; but the French squadron from the Mauritius might be a serviceable ally, especially as communication between the three British presidencies must be mainly carried on by sea. Hyder Ali commenced negotiations with the French. The British in the course of a general seizure of the French trading stations sent troops across Mysore territory to capture the fort of Mahé on the west coast. Hyder Ali considered himself insulted, and in 1780 he suddenly invaded the Carnatic with a horde of savage followers. One body of British troops under Baillie was cut to pieces ; another under Sir Hector Munro was driven in to the forts.

Eyre Coote was dispatched by Warren Hastings from Calcutta, and the veteran checked the tide of disaster but could not crush the enemy. The great French admiral Suffren appeared in the Indian waters, and gradually after a series of stubborn engagements obtained the upper hand by sea. The position of the British garrisons in southern India had now become most precarious. Relief however was brought by the announcement of peace between France and England (1783); the withdrawal of Suffren, following the death of Hyder Ali, made the native powers disinclined to continue the struggle, and so the British power was saved. In this connexion however it must not be forgotten that British fleets had been recently achieving successes which make it probable that, if the French war had continued, naval reinforcements would shortly have arrived in Indian waters, and have neutralised Suffren's predominance, which was never very pronounced.

§ 4. *The Governorship of Bengal, and the Rohilla war.*

In 1772 Warren Hastings became governor of Bengal ; and the brief period which elapsed before his appointment to the post of Governor-General under Lord North's Regulating Act, was marked by useful administrative reforms, and by the action which meets with Macaulay's severest condemnation, the Rohilla war.

In the matter of administration, it was the Governor's wish to get rid of the formal sovereignty of the Nawab, and openly to declare the sovereignty of the Company. Although he could not accomplish this, the method of dealing with the revenue was brought under better control by the removal of Mahomed Reza Khan from the headship of the department; a fresh assessment of the land revenue was carried through ; and a commencement was made of reorganising the administration of justice. It is sufficient here merely to allude to these matters; but the Rohilla affair requires much fuller treatment, since Macaulay has rested upon it a very severe indictment of Hastings's character, while giving what is now recognised as a very misleading account of the whole transaction.

The Rohillas were a group of Afghan or Pathan Mussulmans who during the eighteenth century installed themselves by conquest in the territories upon the western borders of Oude. Though Macaulay speaks of them as mustering 80,000, they do not appear to have really numbered more than some 40,000, Macaulay having misapprehended the statement of the authority he followed. They had not formed themselves into a state till the middle of the century, and then they were at best a body of Mahommedan soldiers who had enforced their rule over a Hindoo population of twenty times their numbers. Rohilcund was not a land made beautiful by the idyllic sway of philosophers and poets, as Macaulay would almost lead one to believe, but a recently conquered country where the ruling race conducted themselves much as ruling races usually do in the East, though the chief at their head happened at the time to be an administrator of ability.

The aggressive attitude of the Mahrattas has already been remarked; and they bore some ill-will to the Rohillas, who had greatly distinguished themselves on the side of Ahmed Shah at the great Mahratta defeat of Paniput. The Mahrattas threatened Rohilcund. The Rohillas appealed to Oude for help, and the Vizier appealed to the English. Help was sent, and the Mahrattas retired.

But when the Vizier demanded payment as promised for the help given, the Rohillas did not respond. The Vizier became convinced that they were playing him false, and were in fact intriguing with the Mahrattas with a view to a combined attack on Oude. Therefore he conceived the plan of crushing the Rohillas by the aid of the British and appropriating their territory.

Throughout his career Hastings was in perpetual difficulties from want of funds, since the normal revenues of Bengal did not meet the requirements of the London Directors, who wanted dividends, although the funds were insufficient to bear the full normal strain of administration, apart from the exceptional strain which the relation of the British to the native states might bring upon them at any time. When Shah Alum ceded the districts of Allahabad and Cora to the Mahrattas, the British (as already related) would not sanction the cession, but reoccupied the country; and by then selling them to Oude for a large sum, at once replenished the coffers of Calcutta and strengthened Oude against the Mahrattas. To complete the treaty with the Nawab-Vizier, Hastings met him at Benares in 1773. The plan of suppressing the Rohillas was then mooted, was agreed to by Hastings, and was put in operation some months later.

The method by which the design was carried out will be dealt with presently; but the policy of suppressing the Rohillas and annexing Rohilcund to Oude, though it may not meet with approval, was certainly not the wholly indefensible thing that Macaulay would have us believe. In his view, a flourishing state was wantonly laid waste, and a noble race annihilated, to satisfy the greed of an Oriental despot and to provide the cash of which the governor was in need. Both the act and the motive are here thoroughly misrepresented.

Was it unjust to the Rohillas to attack them; or to the Hindoo population of Rohilcund to annex them? If not, were there strong reasons which made the annexation desirable? For the first question; the Rohillas were in Rohilcund in virtue of a conquest in which the aggression had been theirs; they had not even been fully established for thirty years; and the very principle which justified their presence in Rohilcund would equally justify a stronger power in ejecting them. In addition to this, the Vizier had just ground of complaint against them for refusing to meet their engagements: and beyond this, he believed that they were actively intriguing against him, and that in self-defence it was necessary to take the offensive. As for the second question, that of the Hindoo population, it was not likely to make much difference to them who their masters were. Oude Nawabs in the long run were not likely to treat them much better or much worse than Pathan chiefs. Coming to the third question; from the British point of view, cash was by no means the only advantage. The maintenance of Oude as a buffer against the Mahrattas was a cardinal point in the political scheme. By the annexation, the Oude frontier would be secured, and what was now accounted a standing menace to Oude would be removed.

Taking all these points into consideration, it seems tolerably clear that if an alliance between Mahrattas and Rohillas had been proved, the justification of annexation would have been indisputable. As it was, the danger to be guarded against was possible, probable perhaps, but not certain; so that it may reasonably be maintained that in supporting the Vizier the British were in effect giving countenance to the theory that the stronger power has a right to conquer the weaker if the latter can be regarded as a merely possible source of danger. In brief, the measure of justification would depend on the degree of well-grounded apprehension: and whether in this case the ground was fully sufficient is a matter on which the evidence is inconclusive.

When we come to the method, however, it is evident that if the British were to have a hand in the subjugation of the Rohillas, they were bound to insist on a European standard of decency in its conduct. But Hastings omitted to make any stipulations on the subject. The result was that on the defeat of the Rohillas the Vizier's troops indulged in grave excesses, and for some time afterwards Champion, the British officer in command, complained that outrages continued which he was powerless to check. His charges, however, were couched in very general terms, and he produced hardly any specific evidence, though repeatedly asked to do so. Both he and the political agent Middleton were instructed to remonstrate against excesses in the strongest terms by Hastings. The universal massacring of Rohillas is reduced by the evidence to the expulsion across the Ganges of those who were under arms, and the whole picture as painted by Macaulay (mainly on the authority of Mill) is proved to be a gross exaggeration. Still, when the best is said that can be urged, the fact remains that while the repeated protests of the British did curb the ghastly license which accompanies the movements of a conquering Oriental army, outrages and excesses were perpetrated which ought to have been foreseen and guarded against by preliminary engagements, and to have been checked by protests more emphatic and more uncompromising than any that were offered.

The policy of the war remains an unsettled question, because its justice is not fully established, while grave blame attaches to Hastings for not taking due order to prevent the excesses by which it was accompanied. But it is untrue that Hastings made light of those excesses, or that he did not protest against them; the lurid picture of outrage and massacre is drawn from wholly insufficient evidence; the extermination of the Rohillas is a fiction; and the description of the war as a mere devastating raid with plunder as its object, in which the Company's troops were let out as mercenaries by way of a cash transaction, is a complete distortion of the real facts, due apparently to Macaulay's acceptance of Mill's version of the affair without further investigation.

§ 5. *Hastings, Impey, and Francis.*

The worst features of the first British government or rather occupancy of Bengal had been remedied by Clive's measures of 1765 and 1766. But the state of administration had continued to be eminently unsatisfactory, numerous tales of misconduct reached England, there was a terrible famine, the evils of which the Company's servants were accused of aggravating; and in the lull between the Wilkes excitements and the final rupture with the American colonies, Parliament found time to investigate Indian affairs. The investigation resulted in Lord North's Regulating Acts of 1773.

These Acts provided that instead of three independent

governors, India should have one Governor-General in Bengal, to whose rule the governments of Madras and Bombay should be subordinated. The Governor-General was to have a Council consisting of four members besides himself, and the vote of a majority of the Council was to be decisive. Hence if three members of the Council set themselves in opposition to the Governor-General, they could carry all their own measures and negative his. Farther, a Supreme Court of Judicature was established consisting of four judges, over whom the Governor and Council had no control, while their actual powers and the extent of their jurisdiction were left undefined.

This arrangement was obviously calculated to encourage perpetual dissensions between the Governor-General, the Council, and the Courts; nor did the composition of the Council and the judges tend to diminish the danger of friction. On the Council, one man experienced in Indian affairs was appointed, Barwell. The other three, Francis, Monson, and General Clavering were appointed, it might almost be said, as a hostile committee. The judges were not men of remarkable ability, and the Chief Justice Impey was not of a conciliatory disposition. And Hastings was Governor-General.

The new members of Calcutta had hardly reached Calcutta (Oct. 1774) when troubles began. Hastings did not receive them with the ceremony they expected, and they began operations by challenging his proceedings in the past and collecting charges against him. The principal agent in the attack was the Brahmin Nuncomar, who supported his allegations against Hastings by the methods of forgery and perjury which are only too familiar in Oriental law-courts. At the very moment when Hastings was brought to bay, his accuser was charged with forgery in an independent case by a native named Mohun Persad. Nuncomar was tried before the four judges of the Supreme Court, was convicted, and was executed in accordance with English law.

Out of the fact that Mohun Persad's attack on Nuncomar was exceedingly opportune for Hastings, Macaulay has constructed a very remarkable picture of Impey in the character of

Judge Jefferies; while Hastings's conduct is excused in terms which amount to a real condemnation. Yet the plain fact is that there is nothing beyond the opportuneness of the charge to connect it with Hastings at all; the charge itself arose out of a suit that had been going on for a long time; the accuser had only just obtained the evidence he required; having obtained it, he at once struck at a man whom he had long been wishing to ruin, the newly-established court giving the opportunity for criminal proceedings. And as concerns Impey; legal opinion at the present day is, that the conviction was in accord with the evidence. The trial took place not before Impey alone but before the whole bench of judges, and they were all in agreement; the proceedings were not hurried, but were conducted with extreme formality; and the Council expressly declined to intercede with the Court for a respite.

It may be added that the picturesque account of the shock produced on the native mind is much overdrawn. The execution of a Brahmin was not an unprecedented horror, since the Mussulmans had no respect for Brahmins, and Bengal had been under Mussulman rulers for several generations.

The fall of Nuncomar stopped the Council's plan of suppressing Hastings by collecting hostile evidence. But in 1775 they found means to effectively thwart his policy. Sujah Dowlah, the Oude Vizier, died; and was succeeded by his son Asaph-ul-Dowlah. The Council proceeded to do all they could to hamper the new Vizier's government by curtailing his sources of revenue. As the price of renewing the treaties which had been made with his father, they insisted on an increase of the subsidies for maintaining the Company's troops in Oude and on the cession of the districts of Ghazipoor and Benares: and they supported and enforced by their own guarantee the claim of the Vizier's mother and grandmother (the Begums of Oude) to retain a quantity of treasure and certain very rich districts for their own advantage. All this was done in the teeth of Hastings.

Farther, they set about systematically reversing the Governor-General's administrative reforms. Thus, the revenue officers had formerly acted also as magistrates; Hastings had gradually substituted regular courts; the Council returned to the old system. So matters went on until Monson's death in 1776 enabled Hastings with Barwell to outvote Francis and Clavering. From that time Hastings really remained predominant. By the time Monson's successor, Wheler, appeared on the scenes, Clavering had died, leaving the balance unaltered; and Eyre Coote, Clavering's successor, at any rate did not make a system of opposing the Governor-General.

Hastings was thus enabled to carry through two measures of importance, one being the establishment of an office for the proper assessment of land and for recording the methods of tenure: while the other was a reconstruction of the terms on which troops were maintained by the Oude Vizier. They were transferred to the Company, to be maintained and officered by the Company, land revenues to cover the cost being assigned to the Company at the same time.

Before proceeding to the affairs of Cheyte Singh and the Begums, the contest between the Council and the Supreme Court requires to be touched on. Except for the inevitable attack upon Impey, towards whose memory Macaulay cherished feelings akin to those which he reserved among his contemporaries for Mr Croker and the Reverend Robert Montgomery, the account in the essay does not require much supplementing. Exaggerations of the judicial enormities will be pointed out in detail in the notes. The position in brief amounted to this, that the judges claimed the power of trying all the officers of the Company, in effect on any charges that anyone might bring against them; whereby administration tended to be brought to a standstill; until the Council, with the sanction of physical force behind them, resisted the orders of the Court, thereby nullifying its power. The only way out of the difficulty was some kind of compromise, since the Court had no means of enforcing its pretensions while it could not simply withdraw them. Hastings devised the plan of giving Impey a supervisory appointment over the district courts as a servant of the Company, subject to the scheme being approved in England.

It is not easy to see where Impey's criminality in accepting the arrangement lies.

The episodes of the resignation of the Governor-Generalship, and of the duel with Francis, are of biographical rather than historical importance, and need not here detain us.

§ 6. *Cheyte Singh and the Oude Begums.*

The affairs of Cheyte Singh, Rajah of Benares, and of the Oude Begums, are both clearly and simply attributable to the need of money under stress of wars which were being carried on in India when England was fighting for life in the West and could render no assistance.

Bulwunt Singh, father of Cheyte Singh, was a landowner to whom the Vizier of Oude had granted the title of Rajah. He paid a large tribute to the Vizier; and on the accession of Asaph-ul-Dowlah, Benares and the tribute were transferred to the Company. The tribute was duly paid; but when the Mahratta war drained the Bengal coffers, Hastings held that he was entitled to demand further contributions from Benares There was no constitutional principle on which the question could be decided, while as far as custom went there was in the East no question of rights wherever might was indisputable. The Rajah paid once, but grew restive when the demand was repeated. Hastings demanded a fine; the Rajah evaded payment. Hastings went to Benares with a small escort, and arrested the Rajah in the midst of his own people. Naturally, the Rajah's adherents rose; the affair assumed the proportions of a revolt, which was however quickly suppressed by the vigour and decision of the Governor-General's action; and Benares was forfeited to the Company.

Macaulay finds it almost incredible that when the proposal of impeaching Warren Hastings came before Parliament, Pitt should have opposed it on the Rohilla question, and have supported it on the Benares question. That he did so is certainly remarkable but not unintelligible. If it be granted that the Rohilla war was honestly regarded as a military necessity for the defence of Oude, it did not afford ground for impeachment. Whereas if it was held, as Pitt seems to have held, that while Hastings was entitled to demand extraordinary aids from Benares, he used that right with the deliberate intention of driving Cheyte Singh to resistance by making demands which he knew to be excessive, the Governor-General's action in that case could only be regarded as a tyrannical abuse of the powers he wielded.

Hastings's treatment of Cheyte Singh was questionable at the best, but it derives some additional justification from the suspicions which were certainly entertained that the Rajah was in fact preparing to take advantage of the attitude of Hyder Ali in Mysore, and of the accumulation of forces hostile to the British in India, to repudiate the Company's domination altogether. In the existing state of affairs it was a reasonable contention that where revolt might be expected it was best to anticipate it by decisive measures of prevention.

The chronic strain on the Treasury was at this time aggravated by the straits in which Asaph-ul-Dowlah found himself. His subsidies to the Company were very much in arrear, and in response to the urgent demands that he should meet his obligations, he could only declare his inability to do so. That his troubles were very largely due to his own maladministration need not be denied; still it was impossible to overlook his contention that the way in which the Company had treated him on his accession really made them responsible for the extent to which his resources were crippled. By the guarantee which the Council had granted in direct opposition to Hastings, a large treasure and a quantity of revenue had been appropriated to the Begums: these ladies were the Vizier's bitter enemies and refused to lend him any assistance.

It was therefore now suggested by Asaph-ul-Dowlah that he could meet his engagements if he was allowed to demand supplies from the Begums, which he would be free to do if the Council withdrew their guarantee. Hastings might argue that the guarantee was not in its nature permanent, and that in withdrawing it he was merely cancelling a measure to which he

had always been opposed; besides which, since the Begums
were suspected of having fomented the insurrection at Benares,
they had forfeited their rights. The pretext was at any rate
sufficiently colourable for a man in such straits for money as
Hastings was; and he gave the required permission. When
the Begums resisted the Vizier, they were declared to be in
rebellion, so justifying the direct intervention of the British. As
in the case of the Rohillas, the Vizier's officers were allowed to
indulge in quite inexcusable severities, this time without protest
and even with the direct countenance of the British. The
treasure and the estates were forfeited, and only a greatly
reduced though by no means despicable allowance was granted
to the Begums.

§ 7. 1785.

In 1785 the Governor-Generalship of Hastings terminated.
In spite of enormous difficulties, he had saved the power
of Great Britain in India and created an administrative
machinery which, imperfect as it necessarily was, was still
founded on sound principles and has remained the basis of our
working system. And this he did though his hand was
constantly forced by the blunders of Madras and Bombay,
though for a time he was actually overruled by his own
Council, though even when he was predominant every step he
took met with the bitterest opposition, though England, fighting
with her back to the wall, could render no assistance, though to
the intolerable strain on his resources was added the Directors'
perpetual demand for larger remittances. In the course of that
desperate struggle, the alternative to raising money by abnormal
and exceptional methods was—retreat before the Mahrattas,
which would have encouraged their aggression; probably
evacuation of the Carnatic with (possibly at least) the re-
instalment there of the French; not improbably, insurrection
in Bengal itself. Under such conditions, men are apt to justify
actions which have no moral excuse, to discover plausible
pretexts which assume the aspect of convincing reasons. That
Hastings dealt unjustly because with insufficient grounds in the

matters of Rohilcund, of Cheyte Singh, of the Begums, most candid readers will recognise : but that he should have honestly persuaded himself of the contrary is so thoroughly intelligible, that an impartial historian can hardly take upon himself to deny it. He saved India, and to do so resorted at times to methods which to the calm observer were at best questionable, but to the man fighting there in India appeared morally defensible, and politically unavoidable. And his reward was—Impeachment.

His retirement was followed by the establishment of the new Constitution framed by Pitt's India Bill, under which India was governed till, after the mutiny of 1857, the government was transferred from the Company to the Crown. By this Bill, a board of control was established in London, which formed a part of the ministry, with a parliamentary head. This body had access to all the correspondence, and supervised the instructions of the board of directors, who could issue their own instructions subject to the approval of the board of control ; so that a direct relation was established between Parliament and the government of India. The Councils of the three presidencies were reduced in numbers, while the Governor-General was granted powers of action on emergency which rendered him practically autocratic ; and the conflict of jurisdictions was removed by abolishing the fiction of the Nawab's sovereignty and declaring the Company sovereign. The first Governor-General sent out under the new system was Lord Cornwallis.

§ 8. *Contemporary events and persons.*

When Warren Hastings began to take an active though subordinate part in Indian affairs, the Seven Years' War was raging in Europe and in Canada : William Pitt was at the head of the English Government, and the naval supremacy of England was being rapidly asserted. When that war came to an end in 1763, George III. had become king with the direct purpose of obtaining the mastery over Parliament, and Pitt had been displaced by the royal favourite Bute.

Bute's ascendency was short-lived, and the section of Whigs headed by Grenville and Portland came into office. In their pedantic attempt to force taxation on the American colonies by the Stamp Act, and in their attack on the demagogue John Wilkes, the ministers' policy was in agreement with the king's; but they succeeded in making themselves so violently obnoxious to him personally that in 1765 they were driven from office; though George was compelled to accept as the alternative another section of the Whigs, headed by the Marquis of Rockingham and inspired by Edmund Burke, whose policy was opposed to his own. But the Rockinghams could not control Parliament, and in 1766 William Pitt was persuaded to form an administration. Unfortunately, he began by accepting the Earldom of Chatham, thereby greatly damaging his own influence: then his health broke down completely; and the ministry, without any real head, plunged into a series of blunders, making the breach with America irreparable and raising violent popular excitement by repeated expulsions of John Wilkes after his election for Middlesex. At last in 1770 the king obtained such a following in Parliament that Lord North became Prime Minister with a majority behind him; and for twelve years North mismanaged the policy of the country at the king's bidding; and, for the greater part of the time, with the support of the country. The result was that war between England and the American colonies broke out in 1775, shortly after the arrival in India of Francis and his colleagues (see § 5).

The war in America was laboriously mismanaged until in the autumn of 1777 Burgoyne's surrender at Saratoga threatened the British arms with complete disaster. In the spring of the next year France declared war in support of the revolted colonies. The British armies obtained no decisive mastery over the Americans; the British fleets could obtain none over the French. In the summer of 1779 Spain threw in her lot with France: Minorca and Gibraltar were blockaded; a great fleet threatened the British Channel: at the end of 1780 the Baltic powers united to resist the British claim to the right of search, and Holland joined the allies against England.

In October 1781 the British forces in America were forced to surrender at Yorktown, and the war with the colonies was practically ended. England seemed to be on the verge of ruin, but was saved in the following year by the brilliant achievements of her navy under Rodney, Hood, and Hawke, and was able to make a peace with her European foes far more favourable than could have been looked for in 1781. But the surrender of York-town had made the continuation of the North ministry impossible : the country had been excited by Lord George Gordon's " No-popery" riots ; a strong reaction had set in against the parliamentary predominance of the king ; and in March 1782 George was obliged, with the bitterest reluctance, to accept a second Rockingham ministry, in which Fox (C. J.) and Shelburne held the leading positions. William Pitt the younger was in the House, but not in the ministry. Rockingham died, and in June Shelburne became Prime Minister. Fox and others of his friends resigned, and virtually went into opposition. The political world was now scandalised by the coalition between North and Fox which drove Shelburne from office in the spring of 1783. The coalition had a large parliamentary majority, but it was unpopular ; when Fox brought in his Bill for the government of India, it was passed in the Commons, but thrown out in the Lords in consequence of the unconstitu-tional interference of the king. In December ministers were turned out of office, Pitt became Prime Minister, while Shelburne practically retired with the title of Marquis of Lansdowne. For three months Pitt fought an adverse majority, then Parliament was dissolved, and Pitt was returned to power with an overwhelming majority (April 1784).

Thus when Hastings returned to England in 1785 Pitt was in the full tide of triumph. His victory was also the victory of the king, who detested Fox, and detested North no less since the coalition. The most notable members of Pitt's cabinet were Dundas and the Lord Chancellor Thurlow. In the Opposition were North, Fox, Sheridan, Burke ; with them was George, Prince of Wales.

Pitt remained at the head of the state until the union with

Ireland in 1801, when he resigned because Catholic Emancipation, to which he had pledged himself, was refused. During that
period, Europe had been thrown into the melting-pot of the
French Revolution. But broadly speaking, after the great
indictments by Burke and Sheridan, the career of Warren
Hastings was unaffected by politics or persons, and this brief
historical outline may here be brought to a close.

III. OF INDIAN TERMS.

It is unfortunate that no kind of uniformity has yet been
arrived at in the spelling of Indian terms. An exceedingly
rough and ready method of adopting a form which broadly
represented their sound was generally acted upon till quite
recently; so that Macaulay talks of the Nabob, or of Surajah
Dowlah, or of Morari Row; just as we are wont to talk of
Aladdin. And just as we resent being required to call that
mythical hero Ala-ud-din, so we resent any novel presentation
of such names as Lucknow or Cawnpore, which have become in
that form a part of the English language. But, setting aside
such thoroughly familiar terms as these, there appears to be
no reason against adopting some system a little more accurate
than the old one. Suraj-ud-daulah, and Morari Rao convey a
more correct impression of sound than Surajah Dowlah and
Morari Row. The only objection is that as long as our spelling
is guided wholly by phonetics, and several different values may
be attached to the same letter, there is very little prospect of a
uniform spelling being arrived at, and "Mahratta" and
"Maratha" will retain an equal authority. This however is
an objection which is valid only if it be admitted that uniformity
is of any real importance.

A practice however has quite recently arisen of discarding
both the old conventional method and the more modern
corrections thereof; and of substituting collocations of letters
with unexpected accents on a fairly uniform but not very
intelligible system. "Arcot" becomes "Arkát"; "Buxar" is
"Báksár"; "Lucknow" is "Lákhnáo"; and this is coming

to be regarded as a sort of authoritative or official spelling, especially since it has been adopted in the " Rulers of India " series issued by the Clarendon Press.

In order to create the minimum of confusion in the reader's mind, I have both in the Introduction and Notes kept almost invariably to the spelling adopted by Macaulay. But I have here appended a list of terms mentioned in this volume, together with the variants under which the reader is likely to find the same persons or places appearing in other volumes dealing with the same subject. But even this list does not exhaust the varieties.

Asaph-ul-Dowlah, Asaf-ud-daula.
Aurungzebe, Aurungzib (Alam-
 gír).
aumil, ámil.
Bahar, Behar.
begum, begam.
Bonsla, Bhonsla.
Carnatic, Karnátik, Karnátak.
Cheyte Sing, Chait Sing, Singh.
Coleroon, Kalrun.
Cora, Corah, Kora.
Cossimbuzar, Kasimbázár.
crore, karor.
Delhi, Dehli.
Fulda, Falta.
Ghizni, Guznee.
Goordas, Gurdás.
Guzerat, Gujerat.
Guicowar, Gaekwar, Gaikwar.
Hoogley, Hooghly, Húglí.
Hyder, Haidar.
Hyderabad, Haidarabad.
jaghire, jagír, jaegír.
lac, lákh.
Lucknow, Lákhnáo.
Mahommed, Mahomet, Muham-
 med, Mohammed.

Mahratta, Maratha, Marhátha.
Meer Jaffier, Mír Jáfar.
Mogul, Moghul, Mughal.
Moorshedabad, Murshedabád.
Mysore, Maisúr.
Nabob, Nawáb, Nuwab.
Nuncomar, Nand Kumár, Nanda-
 Kumár.
nuzzur, nazar.
Oude, Oudh.
perwannah, parwána.
Peshwa, Peishwa.
Pollilore, Polilur.
pundit, pandit.
Punjaub, Punjab, Panjab.
rajah, rájá.
Reza Khan, Raza Khán.
Rohilcund, Rohilkhand.
Scindia, Sindhia, Sindiah.
Sevajee, Sivaji.
Sujah Dowlah, Shujah Daulah,
 Shujah-ud-daula.
sunnud, sanad.
Surajah Dowlah, Suraj-ud-daulah.
vizier, wazír.
zemindar, zamíndár.

WARREN HASTINGS.

THIS book seems to have been manufactured in pursuance
of a contract, by which the representatives of Warren
Hastings, on the one part, bound themselves to furnish
papers, and Mr Gleig, on the other part, bound himself to
furnish praise. It is but just to say that the covenants on 5
both sides have been most faithfully kept; and the result
is before us in the form of three big bad volumes, full of
undigested correspondence and undiscerning panegyric.

If it were worth while to examine this performance in
detail, we could easily make a long article by merely pointing 10
out inaccurate statements, inelegant expressions, and immoral doctrines. But it would be idle to waste criticism on
a bookmaker; and, whatever credit Mr Gleig may have
justly earned by former works, it is as a bookmaker, and
nothing more, that he now comes before us. More eminent 15
men than Mr Gleig have written nearly as ill as he, when
they have stooped to similar drudgery. It would be unjust
to estimate Goldsmith by the History of Greece, or Scott by
the Life of Napoleon. Mr Gleig is neither a Goldsmith nor
a Scott; but it would be unjust to deny that he is capable 20
of something better than these Memoirs. It would also, we

hope and believe, be unjust to charge any Christian minister
with the guilt of deliberately maintaining some propositions
which we find in this book.   It is not too much to say that
Mr Gleig has written several passages, which bear the same
5 relation to the Prince of Machiavelli that the Prince of
Machiavelli bears to the Whole Duty of Man, and which
would excite amazement in a den of robbers, or on board of
a schooner of pirates.   But we are willing to attribute these
offences to haste, to thoughtlessness, and to that disease of
10 the understanding which may be called the *Furor Biographicus*, and which is to writers of lives what the *goître*
is to an Alpine shepherd, or dirt-eating to a Negro slave.

   We are inclined to think that we shall best meet the
wishes of our readers, if, instead of dwelling on the faults
15 of this book, we attempt to give, in a way necessarily hasty
and imperfect, our own view of the life and character of Mr
Hastings.   Our feeling towards him is not exactly that of
the House of Commons which impeached him in 1787 ;
neither is it that of the House of Commons which uncovered
20 and stood up to receive him in 1813.   He had great qualities,
and he rendered great services to the state.   But to repre-
sent him as a man of stainless virtue is to make him
ridiculous ; and from regard for his memory, if from no
other feeling, his friends would have done well to lend no
25 countenance to such puerile adulation.   We believe that, if
he were now living, he would have sufficient judgment and
sufficient greatness of mind to wish to be shown as he was.
He must have known that there were dark spots on his
fame.   He might also have felt with pride that the splendour
30 of his fame would bear many spots.   He would have preferred, we are confident, even the severity of Mr Mill to the
puffing of Mr Gleig.   He would have wished posterity to
have a likeness of him, though an unfavourable likeness,

rather than a daub at once insipid and unnatural, resembling neither him nor any body else. " Paint me as I am," said Oliver Cromwell, while sitting to young Lely. " If you leave out the scars and wrinkles, I will not pay you a shilling." Even in such a trifle, the great Protector showed 5 both his good sense and his magnanimity. He did not wish all that was characteristic in his countenance to be lost, in the vain attempt to give him the regular features and smooth blooming cheeks of the curl-pated minions of James the First. He was content that his face should go forth marked 10 with all the blemishes which had been put on it by time, by war, by sleepless nights, by anxiety, perhaps by remorse; but with valour, policy, authority, and public care written in all its princely lines. If men truly great knew their own interest, it is thus that they would wish their minds to be 15 portrayed.

Warren Hastings sprang from an ancient and illustrious race. It has been affirmed that his pedigree can be traced back to the great Danish sea-king, whose sails were long the terror of both coasts of the British Channel, and who, after 20 many fierce and doubtful struggles, yielded at last to the valour and genius of Alfred. But the undoubted splendour of the line of Hastings needs no illustration from fable. One branch of that line wore, in the fourteenth century, the coronet of Pembroke. From another branch sprang the 25 renowned Chamberlain, the faithful adherent of the White Rose, whose fate has furnished so striking a theme both to poets and to historians. His family received from the Tudors the earldom of Huntingdon, which, after long dispossession, was regained in our time by a series of events 30 scarcely paralleled in romance.

The lords of the manor of Daylesford, in Worcestershire, claimed to be considered as the heads of this distinguished

family.   The main stock, indeed, prospered less than some
of the younger shoots.   But the Daylesford family, though
not ennobled, was wealthy and highly considered, till, about
two hundred years ago, it was overwhelmed by the great
5 ruin of the civil war.   The Hastings of that time was a
zealous cavalier.   He raised money on his lands, sent his
plate to the mint at Oxford, joined the royal army, and,
after spending half his property in the cause of King
Charles, was glad to ransom himself by making over most
10 of the remaining half to Speaker Lenthal.   The old seat at
Daylesford still remained in the family; but it could no
longer be kept up; and in the following generation it was
sold to a merchant of London.

Before this transfer took place, the last Hastings of
15 Daylesford had presented his second son to the rectory of
the parish in which the ancient residence of the family
stood.   The living was of little value; and the situation of
the poor clergyman, after the sale of the estate, was deplor-
able.   He was constantly engaged in lawsuits about his
20 tithes with the new lord of the manor, and was at length
utterly ruined.   His eldest son, Howard, a well-conducted
young man, obtained a place in the Customs.   The second
son, Pynaston, an idle, worthless boy, married before he was
sixteen, lost his wife in two years, and died in the West Indies,
25 leaving to the care of his unfortunate father a little orphan,
destined to strange and memorable vicissitudes of fortune.

Warren, the son of Pynaston, was born on the sixth of
December, 1732.   His mother died a few days later, and he
was left dependent on his distressed grandfather.   The child
30 was early sent to the village school, where he learned his
letters on the same bench with the sons of the peasantry.
Nor did any thing in his garb or fare indicate that his life
was to take a widely different course from that of the young

rustics with whom he studied and played. But no cloud
could overcast the dawn of so much genius and so much
ambition. The very ploughmen observed, and long remembered, how kindly little Warren took to his book. The daily
sight of the lands which his ancestors had possessed, and 5
which had passed into the hands of strangers, filled his
young brain with wild fancies and projects. He loved to
hear stories of the wealth and greatness of his progenitors,
of their splendid housekeeping, their loyalty, and their
valour. On one bright summer day, the boy, then just 10
seven years old, lay on the bank of the rivulet which flows
through the old domain of his house to join the Isis. There,
as threescore and ten years later he told the tale, rose in his
mind a scheme which, through all the turns of his eventful
career, was never abandoned. He would recover the estate 15
which had belonged to his fathers. He would be Hastings
of Daylesford. This purpose, formed in infancy and poverty,
grew stronger as his intellect expanded and as his fortune
rose. He pursued his plan with that calm but indomitable
force of will which was the most striking peculiarity of his 20
character. When, under a tropical sun, he ruled fifty
millions of Asiatics, his hopes, amidst all the cares of war,
finance, and legislation, still pointed to Daylesford. And
when his long public life, so singularly chequered with good
and evil, with glory and obloquy, had at length closed for 25
ever, it was to Daylesford that he retired to die.

When he was eight years old, his uncle Howard determined to take charge of him, and to give him a liberal
education. The boy went up to London, and was sent to
a school at Newington, where he was well taught but ill fed. 30
He always attributed the smallness of his stature to the
hard and scanty fare of this seminary. At ten he was removed to Westminster School, then flourishing under the

care of Dr Nichols.   Vinny Bourne, as his pupils affection-
ately called him, was one of the masters.   Churchill, Colman,
Lloyd, Cumberland, Cowper, were among the students.   With
Cowper, Hastings formed a friendship which neither the
5 lapse of time, nor a wide dissimilarity of opinions and pursuits, could wholly dissolve.   It does not appear that they
ever met after they had grown to manhood.   But forty years
later, when the voices of many great orators were crying for
vengeance on the oppressor of India, the shy and secluded
10 poet could image to himself Hastings the Governor-General
only as the Hastings with whom he had rowed on the
Thames, and played in the cloister, and refused to believe
that so good-tempered a fellow could have done anything
very wrong.   His own life had been spent in praying, musing,
15 and rhyming among the water-lilies of the Ouse.   He had
preserved in no common measure the innocence of childhood.
His spirit had indeed been severely tried, but not by temptations which impelled him to any gross violation of the rules
of social morality.   He had never been attacked by combina-
20 tions of powerful and deadly enemies.   He had never been
compelled to make a choice between innocence and greatness,
between crime and ruin.   Firmly as he held in theory the
doctrine of human depravity, his habits were such that he
was unable to conceive how far from the path of right even
25 kind and noble natures may be hurried by the rage of conflict
and the lust of dominion.

Hastings had another associate at Westminster of whom
we shall have occasion to make frequent mention, Elijah
Impey.   We know little about their school days.   But, we
30 think, we may safely venture to guess that, whenever
Hastings wished to play any trick more than usually
naughty, he hired Impey with a tart or a ball to act as
fag in the worst part of the prank.

Warren was distinguished among his comrades as an excellent swimmer, boatman, and scholar. At fourteen he was first in the examination for the foundation. His name in gilded letters on the walls of the dormitory still attests his victory over many older competitors. He stayed two years 5 longer at the school, and was looking forward to a studentship at Christ Church, when an event happened which changed the whole course of his life. Howard Hastings died, bequeathing his nephew to the care of a friend and distant relation, named Chiswick. This gentleman, though 10 he did not absolutely refuse the charge, was desirous to rid himself of it as soon as possible. Dr Nichols made strong remonstrances against the cruelty of interrupting the studies of a youth who seemed likely to be one of the first scholars of the age. He even offered to bear the expense of sending 15 his favourite pupil to Oxford. But Mr Chiswick was inflexible. He thought the years which had already been wasted on hexameters and pentameters quite sufficient. He had it in his power to obtain for the lad a writership in the service of the East India Company. Whether the young 20 adventurer, when once shipped off, made a fortune, or died of a liver complaint, he equally ceased to be a burden to anybody. Warren was accordingly removed from Westminster School, and placed for a few months at a commercial academy to study arithmetic and book-keeping. In January, 1750, a 25 few days after he had completed his seventeenth year, he sailed for Bengal, and arrived at his destination in the October following.

He was immediately placed at a desk in the Secretary's office at Calcutta, and laboured there during two years. Fort 30 William was then a purely commercial settlement. In the south of India the encroaching policy of Dupleix had transformed the servants of the English Company, against their

will, into diplomatists and generals. The war of the succession was raging in the Carnatic; and the tide had been suddenly turned against the French by the genius of young Robert Clive. But in Bengal the European settlers, at peace
5 with the natives and with each other, were wholly occupied with ledgers and bills of lading.

After two years passed in keeping accounts at Calcutta, Hastings was sent up the country to Cossimbazar, a town which lies on the Hoogley, about a mile from Moorshedabad,
10 and which then bore to Moorshedabad a relation, if we may compare small things with great, such as the city of London bears to Westminster. Moorshedabad was the abode of the prince who, by an authority ostensibly derived from the Mogul, but really independent, ruled the three great pro-
15 vinces of Bengal, Orissa, and Bahar. At Moorshedabad were the court, the haram, and the public offices. Cossimbazar was a port and a place of trade, renowned for the quantity and excellence of the silks which were sold in its marts, and constantly receiving and sending forth fleets of richly laden
20 barges. At this important point the Company had established a small factory subordinate to that of Fort William. Here, during several years, Hastings was employed in making bargains for stuffs with native brokers. While he was thus engaged, Surajah Dowlah succeeded to the government, and
25 declared war against the English. The defenceless settlement of Cossimbazar, lying close to the tyrant's capital, was instantly seized. Hastings was sent a prisoner to Moorshedabad, but, in consequence of the humane intervention of the servants of the Dutch Company, was treated with indulgence.
30 Meanwhile the Nabob marched on Calcutta; the governor and the commandant fled; the town and citadel were taken, and most of the English prisoners perished in the Black Hole.

In these events originated the greatness of Warren
Hastings. The fugitive governor and his companions had
taken refuge on the dreary islet of Fulda, near the mouth of
the Hoogley. They were naturally desirous to obtain full
information respecting the proceedings of the Nabob ; and 5
no person seemed so likely to furnish it as Hastings, who
was a prisoner at large in the immediate neighbourhood of
the court. He thus became a diplomatic agent, and soon
established a high character for ability and resolution. The
treason which at a later period was fatal to Surajah Dowlah 10
was already in progress ; and Hastings was admitted to the
deliberations of the conspirators. But the time for striking
had not arrived. It was necessary to postpone the execution
of the design ; and Hastings, who was now in extreme peril,
fled to Fulda.   15

Soon after his arrival at Fulda, the expedition from
Madras, commanded by Clive, appeared in the Hoogley.
Warren, young, intrepid, and excited probably by the example of the Commander of the forces who, having like
himself been a mercantile agent of the Company, had been 20
turned by public calamities into a soldier, determined to
serve in the ranks. During the early operations of the war
he carried a musket. But the quick eye of Clive soon
perceived that the head of the young volunteer would be
more useful than his arm. When, after the battle of Plassey, 25
Meer Jaffier was proclaimed Nabob of Bengal, Hastings was
appointed to reside at the court of the new prince as agent
for the Company.

He remained at Moorshedabad till the year 1761, when
he became a member of Council, and was consequently 30
forced to reside at Calcutta. This was during the interval
between Clive's first and second administration, an interval
which has left on the fame of the East India Company a

stain, not wholly effaced by many years of just and humane government. Mr Vansittart, the Governor, was at the head of a new and anomalous empire. On the one side was a band of English functionaries, daring, intelligent, eager 5 to be rich. On the other side was a great native population, helpless, timid, accustomed to crouch under oppression. To keep the stronger race from preying on the weaker was an undertaking which tasked to the utmost the talents and energy of Clive. Vansittart, with fair intentions, was 10 a feeble and inefficient ruler. The master caste, as was natural, broke loose from all restraint; and then was seen what we believe to be the most frightful of all spectacles, the strength of civilisation without its mercy. To all other despotism there is a check, imperfect indeed, and liable to 15 gross abuse, but still sufficient to preserve society from the last extreme of misery. A time comes when the evils of submission are obviously greater than those of resistance, when fear itself begets a sort of courage, when a convulsive burst of popular rage and despair warns tyrants not to 20 presume too far on the patience of mankind. But against misgovernment such as then afflicted Bengal it was impossible to struggle. The superior intelligence and energy of the dominant class made their power irresistible. A war of Bengalees against Englishmen was like a war of sheep 25 against wolves, of men against dæmons. The only protection which the conquered could find was in the moderation, the clemency, the enlarged policy of the conquerors. That protection, at a later period, they found. But at first English power came among them unaccompanied by English 30 morality. There was an interval between the time at which they became our subjects, and the time at which we began to reflect that we were bound to discharge towards them the duties of rulers. During that interval the business of a

servant of the Company was simply to wring out of the
natives a hundred or two hundred thousand pounds as
speedily as possible, that he might return home before his
constitution had suffered from the heat, to marry a peer's
daughter, to buy rotten boroughs in Cornwall, and to give 5
balls in St James's Square. Of the conduct of Hastings at
this time, little is known ; but the little that is known, and
the circumstance that little is known, must be considered
as honourable to him. He could not protect the natives :
all that he could do was to abstain from plundering and 10
oppressing them ; and this he appears to have done. It is
certain that at this time he continued poor; and it is equally
certain, that by cruelty and dishonesty he might easily have
become rich. It is certain that he was never charged with
having borne a share in the worst abuses which then pre- 15
vailed ; and it is almost equally certain that, if he had borne
a share in those abuses, the able and bitter enemies who
afterwards persecuted him would not have failed to discover
and to proclaim his guilt. The keen, severe, and even
malevolent scrutiny to which his whole public life was 20
subjected, a scrutiny unparalleled, as we believe, in the
history of mankind, is in one respect advantageous to his
reputation. It brought many lamentable blemishes to light ;
but it entitles him to be considered pure from every blemish
which has not been brought to light. 25

The truth is that the temptations to which so many
English functionaries yielded in the time of Mr Vansittart
were not temptations addressed to the ruling passions of
Warren Hastings. He was not squeamish in pecuniary
transactions ; but he was neither sordid nor rapacious. 30
He was far too enlightened a man to look on a great empire
merely as a buccaneer would look on a galleon. Had his
heart been much worse than it was, his understanding

would have preserved him from that extremity of baseness.
He was an unscrupulous, perhaps an unprincipled statesman;
but still he was a statesman, and not a freebooter.

In 1764 Hastings returned to England.   He had realized
5 only a very moderate fortune; and that moderate fortune
was soon reduced to nothing, partly by his praiseworthy
liberality, and partly by his mismanagement.   Towards his
relations he appears to have acted very generously.   The
greater part of his savings he left in Bengal, hoping probably
10 to obtain the high usury of India.   But high usury and
bad security generally go together; and Hastings lost both
interest and principal.

He remained four years in England.   Of his life at this
time very little is known.   But it has been asserted, and
15 is highly probable, that liberal studies and the society of
men of letters occupied a great part of his time.   It is to
be remembered to his honour, that in days when the
languages of the East were regarded by other servants of
·the Company merely as the means of communicating with
20 weavers and money-changers, his enlarged and accomplished
mind sought in Asiatic learning for new forms of intellectual
enjoyment, and for new views of government and society.
Perhaps, like most persons who have paid much attention
to departments of knowledge which lie out of the common
25 track, he was inclined to overrate the value of his favourite
studies.   He conceived that the cultivation of Persian
literature might with advantage be made a part of the
liberal education of an English gentleman; and he drew up
a plan with that view.   It is said that the University of
30 Oxford, in which Oriental learning had never, since the
revival of letters, been wholly neglected, was to be the seat
of the institution which he contemplated.   An endowment
was expected from the munificence of the Company; and

professors thoroughly competent to interpret Hafiz. and Ferdusi were to be engaged in the East. Hastings called on Johnson, with the hope, as it should seem, of interesting in this project a man who enjoyed the highest literary reputation, and who was particularly connected with Oxford. 5 The interview appears to have left on Johnson's mind a most favourable impression of the talents and attainments of his visitor. Long after, when Hastings was ruling the immense population of British India, the old philosopher wrote to him, and referred in the most courtly terms, though 10 with great dignity, to their short but agreeable intercourse.

Hastings soon began to look again towards India. He had little to attach him to England; and his pecuniary embarrassments were great. He solicited his old masters the Directors for employment. They acceded to his request, 15 with high compliments both to his abilities and to his integrity, and appointed him a Member of Council at Madras. It would be unjust not to mention that, though forced to borrow money for his outfit, he did not withdraw any portion of the sum which he had appropriated to the 20 relief of his distressed relations. In the spring of 1769 he embarked on board of the Duke of Grafton and commenced a voyage distinguished by incidents which might furnish matter for a novel.

Among the passengers in the Duke of Grafton was a 25 German of the name of Imhoff. He called himself a baron; but he was in distressed circumstances, and was going out to Madras as a portrait-painter, in the hope of picking up some of the pagodas which were then lightly got and as lightly spent by the English in India. The baron was 30 accompanied by his wife, a native, we have somewhere read, of Archangel. This young woman who, born under the Arctic circle, was destined to play the part of a queen

under the tropic of Cancer, had an agreeable person, a cultivated mind, and manners in the highest degree engaging. She despised her husband heartily, and, as the story which we have to tell sufficiently proves, not without
5 reason. She was interested by the conversation and flattered by the attentions of Hastings. The situation was indeed perilous. No place is so propitious to the formation either of close friendships or of deadly enmities as an Indiaman. There are very few people who do not find a voyage which
10 lasts several months insupportably dull. Any thing is welcome which may break that long monotony, a sail, a shark, an albatross, a man overboard. Most passengers find some resource in eating twice as many meals as on land. But the great devices for killing the time are quar-
15 relling and flirting. The facilities for both these exciting pursuits are great. The inmates of the ship are thrown together far more than in any country-seat or boarding-house. None can escape from the rest except by imprisoning himself in a cell in which he can hardly turn. All food, all
20 exercise, is taken in company. Ceremony is to a great extent banished. It is every day in the power of a mischievous person to inflict innumerable annoyances; it is every day in the power of an amiable person to confer little services. It not seldom happens that serious distress and danger call
25 forth in genuine beauty and deformity heroic virtues and abject vices which, in the ordinary intercourse of good society, might remain during many years unknown even to intimate associates. Under such circumstances met Warren Hastings and the Baroness Imhoff, two persons whose ac-
30 complishments would have attracted notice in any court of Europe. The gentleman had no domestic ties. The lady was tied to a husband for whom she had no regard, and who had no regard for his own honour. An attachment

sprang up, which was soon strengthened by events such as
could hardly have occurred on land. Hastings fell ill. The
baroness nursed him with womanly tenderness, gave him his
medicines with her own hand, and even sat up in his cabin
while he slept. Long before the Duke of Grafton reached 5
Madras, Hastings was in love. But his love was of a
most characteristic description. Like his hatred, like his
ambition, like all his passions, it was strong, but not
impetuous. It was calm, deep, earnest, patient of delay,
unconquerable by time. Imhoff was called into council by 10
his wife and his wife's lover. It was arranged that the
baroness should institute a suit for a divorce in the courts of
Franconia, that the baron should afford every facility to the
proceeding, and that, during the years which might elapse
before the sentence should be pronounced, they should 15
continue to live together. It was also agreed that Hastings
should bestow some very substantial marks of gratitude on
the complaisant husband, and should, when the marriage
was dissolved, make the lady his wife, and adopt the
children whom she had already borne to Imhoff.   20

We are not inclined to judge either Hastings or the
baroness severely. There was undoubtedly much to extenuate their fault. But we can by no means concur with
the Reverend Mr Gleig, who carries his partiality to so
injudicious an extreme as to describe the conduct of Imhoff, 25
conduct the baseness of which is the best excuse for the
lovers, as "wise and judicious."

At Madras, Hastings found the trade of the Company in
a very disorganised state. His own tastes would have led
him rather to political than to commercial pursuits: but he 30
knew that the favour of his employers depended chiefly on
their dividends, and that their dividends depended chiefly
on the investment. He therefore, with great judgment,

determined to apply his vigorous mind for a time to this
department of business, which had been much neglected,
since the servants of the Company had ceased to be clerks,
and had become warriors and negotiators.

5   In a very few months he effected an important reform.
The Directors notified to him their high approbation, and
were so much pleased with his conduct that they determined
to place him at the head of the government of Bengal.
Early in 1772 he quitted Fort St George for his new post.
10 The Imhoffs, who were still man and wife, accompanied
him, and lived at Calcutta " on the same wise and judicious
plan,"—we quote the words of Mr Gleig,—which they had
already followed during more than two years.

When Hastings took his seat at the head of the council-
15 board, Bengal was still governed according to the system
which Clive had devised, a system which was, perhaps,
skilfully contrived for the purpose of facilitating and con-
cealing a great revolution, but which, when that revolution
was complete and irrevocable, could produce nothing but
20 inconvenience. There were two governments, the real and
the ostensible. The supreme power belonged to the Company, and was in truth the most despotic power that can be
conceived. The only restraint on the English masters of
the country was that which their own justice and humanity
25 imposed on them. There was no constitutional check on
their will, and resistance to them was utterly hopeless.

But, though thus absolute in reality, the English had
not yet assumed the style of sovereignty. They held their
territories as vassals of the throne of Delhi; they raised
30 their revenues as collectors appointed by the imperial com-
mission; their public seal was inscribed with the imperial
titles; and their mint struck only the imperial coin.

There was still a nabob of Bengal, who stood to the

English rulers of his country in the same relation in which Augustulus stood to Odoacer, or the last Merovingians to Charles Martel and Pepin. He lived at Moorshedabad, surrounded by princely magnificence. He was approached with outward marks of reverence, and his name was used in 5 public instruments. But in the government of the country he had less real share than the youngest writer or cadet in the Company's service.

The English council which represented the Company at Calcutta was constituted on a very different plan from that 10 which has since been adopted. At present the Governor is, as to all executive measures, absolute. He can declare war, conclude peace, appoint public functionaries or remove them, in opposition to the unanimous sense of those who sit with him in council. They are, indeed, entitled to know all that 15 is done, to discuss all that is done, to advise, to remonstrate, to send protests to England. But it is with the Governor that the supreme power resides, and on him that the whole responsibility rests. This system, which was introduced by Mr Pitt and Mr Dundas in spite of the strenuous opposi- 20 tion of Mr Burke, we conceive to be on the whole the best that was ever devised for the government of a country where no materials can be found for a representative constitution. In the time of Hastings the Governor had only one vote in council, and, in case of an equal division, a casting vote. It 25 therefore happened not unfrequently that he was overruled on the gravest questions; and it was possible that he might be wholly excluded, for years together, from the real direction of public affairs.

The English functionaries at Fort William had as yet 30 paid little or no attention to the internal government of Bengal. The only branch of politics about which they much busied themselves was negotiation with the native

princes.   The police, the administration of justice, the
details of the collection of revenue they almost entirely
neglected.   We may remark that the phraseology of the
Company's servants still bears the traces of this state of
5 things.   To this day they always use the word "political" as
synonymous with "diplomatic."   We could name a gentleman still living who was described by the highest authority
as an invaluable public servant, eminently fit to be at the
head of the internal administration of a whole presidency,
10 but unfortunately quite ignorant of all political business.

The internal government of Bengal the English rulers
delegated to a great native minister, who was stationed at
Moorshedabad.   All military affairs, and, with the exception
of what pertains to mere ceremonial, all foreign affairs, were
15 withdrawn from his control; but the other departments of
the administration were entirely confided to him.   His own
stipend amounted to near a hundred thousand pounds
sterling a year.   The personal allowance of the nabobs,
amounting to more than three hundred thousand pounds a
20 year, passed through the minister's hands, and was, to a
great extent, at his disposal.   The collection of the revenue,
the administration of justice, the maintenance of order, were
left to this high functionary; and for the exercise of his
immense power he was responsible to none but the British
25 masters of the country.

A situation so important, lucrative, and splendid, was
naturally an object of ambition to the ablest and most
powerful natives.   Clive had found it difficult to decide
between conflicting pretensions.   Two candidates stood out
30 prominently from the crowd, each of them the representative of a race and of a religion.

The one was Mahommed Reza Khan, a Mussulman of
Persian extraction, able, active, religious after the fashion of

his people, and highly esteemed by them. In England he might perhaps have been regarded as a corrupt and greedy politician. But, tried by the lower standard of Indian morality, he might be considered as a man of integrity and honour. 5

His competitor was a Hindoo Brahmin whose name has, by a terrible and melancholy event, been inseparably associated with that of Warren Hastings, the Maharajah Nuncomar. This man had played an important part in all the revolutions which, since the time of Surajah Dowlah, had 10 taken place in Bengal. To the consideration which in that country belongs to high and pure caste, he added the weight which is derived from wealth, talents, and experience. Of his moral character it is difficult to give a notion to those who are acquainted with human nature only as it appears 15 in our island. What the Italian is to the Englishman, what the Hindoo is to the Italian, what the Bengalee is to other Hindoos, that was Nuncomar to other Bengalees. The physical organization of the Bengalee is feeble even to effeminacy. He lives in a constant vapour bath. His 20 pursuits are sedentary, his limbs delicate, his movements languid. During many ages he has been trampled upon by men of bolder and more hardy breeds. Courage, independence, veracity, are qualities to which his constitution and his situation are equally unfavourable. His mind 25 bears a singular analogy to his body. It is weak even to helplessness, for purposes of manly resistance; but its suppleness and its tact move the children of sterner climates to admiration not unmingled with contempt. All those arts which are the natural defence of the weak are more familiar 30 to this subtle race than to the Ionian of the time of Juvenal, or to the Jew of the dark ages. What the horns are to the buffalo, what the paw is to the tiger, what the sting is to the

bee, what beauty, according to the old Greek song, is to
woman, deceit is to the Bengalee. Large promises, smooth
excuses, elaborate tissues of circumstantial falsehood, chica-
nery, perjury, forgery, are the weapons, offensive and defen-
5 sive, of the people of the Lower Ganges. All those millions
do not furnish one sepoy to the armies of the Company.
But as usurers, as money-changers, as sharp legal practitioners, no class of human beings can bear a comparison
with them. With all his softness, the Bengalee is by no
10 means placable in his enmities or prone to pity. The
pertinacity with which he adheres to his purposes yields only
to the immediate pressure of fear. Nor does he lack a
certain kind of courage which is often wanting in his
masters. To inevitable evils he is sometimes found to
15 oppose a passive fortitude, such as the Stoics attributed to
their ideal sage. An European warrior who rushes on a
battery of cannon with a loud hurrah will sometimes shriek
under the surgeon's knife, and fall into an agony of despair
at the sentence of death. But the Bengalee who would see
20 his country overrun, his house laid in ashes, his children
murdered or dishonoured, without having the spirit to strike
one blow, has yet been known to endure torture with the
firmness of Mucius, and to mount the scaffold with the
steady step and even pulse of Algernon Sydney.

25   In Nuncomar, the national character was strongly and
with exaggeration personified. The Company's servants had
repeatedly detected him in the most criminal intrigues. On
one occasion he brought a false charge against another
Hindoo, and tried to substantiate it by producing forged
30 documents. On another occasion it was discovered that
while professing the strongest attachment to the English,
he was engaged in several conspiracies against them, and in
particular that he was the medium of a correspondence

between the court of Delhi and the French authorities in
the Carnatic.   For these and similar practices he had been
long detained in confinement.   But his talents and influence
had not only procured his liberation, but had obtained for
him a certain degree of consideration even among the British 5
rulers of his country.

Clive was extremely unwilling to place a Mussulman at
the head of the administration of Bengal.   On the other
hand, he could not bring himself to confer immense power
on a man to whom every sort of villany had repeatedly been 10
brought home.   Therefore, though the nabob, over whom
Nuncomar had by intrigue acquired great influence, begged
that the artful Hindoo might be intrusted with the government, Clive, after some hesitation, decided honestly and
wisely in favour of Mahommed Reza Khan, who had held 15
his high office seven years when Hastings became Governor.
An infant son of Meer Jaffier was now nabob; and the
guardianship of the young prince's person had been confided
to the minister.

Nuncomar, stimulated at once by cupidity and malice, 20
had been constantly attempting to undermine his successful
rival.   This was not difficult.   The revenues of Bengal,
under the administration established by Clive, did not yield
such a surplus as had been anticipated by the Company;
for, at that time, the most absurd notions were entertained 25
in England respecting the wealth of India.   Palaces of
porphyry, hung with the richest brocade, heaps of pearls
and diamonds, vaults from which pagodas and gold mohurs
were measured out by the bushel, filled the imagination
even of men of business.   Nobody seemed to be aware of 30
what nevertheless was most undoubtedly the truth, that
India was a poorer country than countries which in Europe
are reckoned poor, than Ireland, for example, or than Por-

tugal. It was confidently believed by lords of the treasury
and members for the city that Bengal would not only defray
its own charges, but would afford an increased dividend
to the proprietors of India stock, and large relief to the
5 English finances.   These absurd expectations were disappointed; and the directors, naturally enough, chose to
attribute the disappointment rather to the mismanagement
of Mahommed Reza Khan than to their own ignorance of
the country intrusted to their care. They were confirmed in
10 their error by the agents of Nuncomar; for Nuncomar had
agents even in Leadenhall Street. Soon after Hastings
reached Calcutta, he received a letter addressed by the
Court of Directors, not to the Council generally, but to
himself in particular.   He was directed to remove Mahom-
15 med Reza Khan, to arrest him, together with all his family
and all his partisans, and to institute a strict inquiry into the
whole administration of the province. It was added that
the Governor would do well to avail himself of the assistance
of Nuncomar in the investigation.   The vices of Nuncomar
20 were acknowledged.   But even from his vices, it was said,
much advantage might at such a conjuncture be derived;
and, though he could not safely be trusted, it might still be
proper to encourage him by hopes of reward.

The Governor bore no good will to Nuncomar.   Many
25 years before, they had known each other at Moorshedabad;
and then a quarrel had risen between them which all the
authority of their superiors could hardly compose. Widely
as they differed in most points, they resembled each other
in this, that both were men of unforgiving natures.   To
30 Mahommed Reza Khan, on the other hand, Hastings had
no feelings of hostility.   Nevertheless he proceeded to
execute the instructions of the Company with an alacrity
which he never showed, except when instructions were in

perfect conformity with his own views. He had, wisely as
we think, determined to get rid of the system of double
government in Bengal. The orders of the directors furnished
him with the means of effecting his purpose, and dispensed
him from the necessity of discussing the matter with his 5
council. He took his measures with his usual vigour and
dexterity. At midnight, the palace of Mahommed Reza
Khan at Moorshedabad was surrounded by a battalion of
sepoys. The minister was roused from his slumbers, and
informed that he was a prisoner. With the Mussulman 10
gravity, he bent his head and submitted himself to the will
of God. He fell not alone. A chief named Schitab Roy
had been intrusted with the government of Bahar. His
valour and his attachment to the English had more than
once been signally proved. On that memorable day on 15
which the people of Patna saw from their walls the whole
army of the Mogul scattered by the little band of Captain
Knox, the voice of the British conquerors assigned the palm
of gallantry to the brave Asiatic. "I never," said Knox,
when he introduced Schitab Roy, covered with blood and 20
dust, to the English functionaries assembled in the factory,
"I never saw a native fight so before." Schitab Roy was
involved in the ruin of Mahommed Reza Khan, was removed
from office, and was placed under arrest. The members of
the council received no intimation of these measures till the 25
prisoners were on their road to Calcutta.

The inquiry into the conduct of the minister was postponed on different pretences. He was detained in an easy
confinement during many months. In the mean time, the
great revolution which Hastings had planned was carried 30
into effect. The office of minister was abolished. The
internal administration was transferred to the servants of the
Company. A system, a very imperfect system, it is true, of

civil and criminal justice, under English superintendence,
was established. The nabob was no longer to have even
an ostensible share in the government; but he was still to
receive a considerable annual allowance, and to be sur-
5 rounded with the state of sovereignty. As he was an infant,
it was necessary to provide guardians for his person and
property. His person was intrusted to a lady of his father's
haram, known by the name of the Munny Begum. The
office of treasurer of the household was bestowed on a son
10 of Nuncomar, named Goordas. Nuncomar's services were
wanted, yet he could not safely be trusted with power; and
Hastings thought it a masterstroke of policy to reward the able
and unprincipled parent by promoting the inoffensive child.

The revolution completed, the double government dis-
15 solved, the Company installed in the full sovereignty of
Bengal, Hastings had no motive to treat the late ministers
with rigour. Their trial had been put off on various pleas
till the new organization was complete. They were then
brought before a committee, over which the Governor pre-
20 sided. Schitab Roy was speedily acquitted with honour.
A formal apology was made to him for the restraint to
which he had been subjected. All the Eastern marks of
respect were bestowed on him. He was clothed in a robe
of state, presented with jewels and with a richly harnessed
25 elephant, and sent back to his government at Patna. But
his health had suffered from confinement; his high spirit
had been cruelly wounded; and soon after his liberation he
died of a broken heart.

The innocence of Mahommed Reza Khan was not so
30 clearly established. But the Governor was not disposed to
deal harshly. After a long hearing, in which Nuncomar
appeared as the accuser, and displayed both the art and the
inveterate rancour which distinguished him, Hastings pro-

nounced that the charges had not been made out, and
ordered the fallen minister to be set at liberty.

Nuncomar had purposed to destroy the Mussulman administration, and to rise on its ruin.   Both his malevolence
and his cupidity had been disappointed. Hastings had made 5
him a tool, had used him for the purpose of accomplishing
the transfer of the government from Moorshedabad to Calcutta, from native to European hands. The rival, the enemy,
so long envied, so implacably persecuted, had been dismissed
unhurt.   The situation so long and ardently desired had 10
been abolished.   It was natural that the Governor should
be from that time an object of the most intense hatred to
the vindictive Brahmin.   As yet, however, it was necessary
to suppress such feelings.   The time was coming when that
long animosity was to end in a desperate and deadly 15
struggle.

In the mean time, Hastings was compelled to turn his
attention to foreign affairs.   The object of his diplomacy
was at this time simply to get money.   The finances of his
government were in an embarrassed state ; and this embar- 20
rassment he was determined to relieve by some means, fair
or foul.   The principle which directed all his dealings with
his neighbours is fully expressed by the old motto of one of
the great predatory families of Teviotdale, "Thou shalt want
ere I want."   He seems to have laid it down, as a funda- 25
mental proposition which could not be disputed, that, when
he had not as many lacs of rupees as the public service
required, he was to take them from any body who had.
One thing, indeed, is to be said in excuse for him.   The
pressure applied to him by his employers at home, was such 30
as only the highest virtue could have withstood, such as left
him no choice except to commit great wrongs, or to resign
his high post, and with that post all his hopes of fortune

and distinction. The directors, it is true, never enjoined or
applauded any crime. Far from it. Whoever examines
their letters written at that time will find there many just
and humane sentiments, many excellent precepts, in short,
5 an admirable code of political ethics. But every exhortation
is modified or nullified by a demand for money. "Govern
leniently, and send more money; practise strict justice and
moderation towards neighbouring powers, and send more
money;" this is in truth the sum of almost all the instruc-
10 tions that Hastings ever received from home. Now these
instructions, being interpreted, mean simply, "Be the father
and the oppressor of the people; be just and unjust,
moderate and rapacious." The directors dealt with India,
as the church, in the good old times, dealt with a heretic.
15 They delivered the victim over to the executioners, with an
earnest request that all possible tenderness might be shown.
We by no means accuse or suspect those who framed these
despatches of hypocrisy. It is probable that, writing fifteen
thousand miles from the place where their orders were to be
20 carried into effect, they never perceived the gross inconsistency of which they were guilty. But the inconsistency
was at once manifest to their lieutenant at Calcutta, who,
with an empty treasury, with an unpaid army, with his own
salary often in arrear, with deficient crops, with government
25 tenants daily running away, was called upon to remit home
another half million without fail. Hastings saw that it was
absolutely necessary for him to disregard either the moral
discourses or the pecuniary requisitions of his employers.
Being forced to disobey them in something, he had to
30 consider what kind of disobedience they would most readily
pardon; and he correctly judged that the safest course would
be to neglect the sermons and to find the rupees.

A mind so fertile as his, and so little restrained by

conscientious scruples, speedily discovered several modes of relieving the financial embarrassments of the government. The allowance of the Nabob of Bengal was reduced at a stroke from three hundred and twenty thousand pounds a year to half that sum. The Company had bound itself to 5 pay near three hundred thousand pounds a year to the great Mogul, as a mark of homage for the provinces which he had intrusted to their care; and they had ceded to him the districts of Corah and Allahabad. On the plea that the Mogul was not really independent, but merely a tool in the 10 hands of others, Hastings determined to retract these concessions. He accordingly declared that the English would pay no more tribute, and sent troops to occupy Allahabad and Corah. The situation of these places was such, that there would be little advantage and great expense in retain- 15 ing them. Hastings, who wanted money and not territory, determined to sell them. A purchaser was not wanting. The rich province of Oude had, in the general dissolution of the Mogul Empire, fallen to the share of the great Mussulman house by which it is still governed. About 20 twenty years ago, this house, by the permission of the British government, assumed the royal title; but, in the time of Warren Hastings, such an assumption would have been considered by the Mahommedans of India as a monstrous impiety. The Prince of Oude, though he held 25 the power, did not venture to use the style of sovereignty. To the appellation of Nabob or Viceroy, he added that of Vizier of the monarchy of Hindostan, just as in the last century the Electors of Saxony and Brandenburg, though independent of the Emperor, and often in arms against him, 30 were proud to style themselves his Grand Chamberlain and Grand Marshal. Sujah Dowlah, then Nabob Vizier, was on excellent terms with the English. He had a large treasure.

Allahabad and Corah were so situated that they might be of
use to him and could be of none to the Company. The
buyer and seller soon came to an understanding; and the
provinces which had been torn from the Mogul were made
5 over to the government of Oude for about half a million
sterling.

But there was another matter still more important to be
settled by the Vizier and the Governor. The fate of a brave
people was to be decided. It was decided in a manner
10 which has left a lasting stain on the fame of Hastings and
of England.

The people of Central Asia had always been to the
inhabitants of India what the warriors of the German forests
were to the subjects of the decaying monarchy of Rome.
15 The dark, slender, and timid Hindoo shrank from a conflict
with the strong muscle and resolute spirit of the fair race,
which dwelt beyond the passes. There is reason to believe
that, at a period anterior to the dawn of regular history, the
people who spoke the rich and flexible Sanscrit came from
20 regions lying far beyond the Hyphasis and the Hystaspes,
and imposed their yoke on the children of the soil. It is
certain that, during the last ten centuries, a succession of
invaders descended from the west on Hindostan : nor was
the course of conquest ever turned back towards the setting
25 sun, till that memorable campaign in which the cross of
Saint George was planted on the walls of Ghizni.

The Emperors of Hindostan themselves came from the
other side of the great mountain ridge; and it had always
been their practice to recruit their army from the hardy and
30 valiant race from which their own illustrious house sprang.
Among the military adventurers who were allured to the
Mogul standards from the neighbourhood of Cabul and
Candahar, were conspicuous several gallant bands, known

by the name of the Rohillas. Their services had been
rewarded with large tracts of land, fiefs of the spear, if we
may use an expression drawn from an analogous state of
things, in that fertile plain through which the Ramgunga
flows from the snowy heights of Kumaon to join the Ganges. 5
In the general confusion which followed the death of Aurungzebe, the warlike colony became virtually independent.
The Rohillas were distinguished from the other inhabitants
of India by a peculiarly fair complexion. They were more
honourably distinguished by courage in war, and by skill in 10
the arts of peace. While anarchy raged from Lahore to
Cape Comorin, their little territory enjoyed the blessings of
repose under the guardianship of valour. Agriculture and
commerce flourished among them; nor were they negligent
of rhetoric and poetry. Many persons now living have heard 15
aged men talk with regret of the golden days when the
Afghan princes ruled in the vale of Rohilcund.

Sujah Dowlah had set his heart on adding this rich
district to his own principality. Right, or show of right, he
had absolutely none. His claim was in no respect better 20
founded than that of Catherine to Poland, or that of the
Bonaparte family to Spain. The Rohillas held their country
by exactly the same title by which he held his, and had
governed their country far better than his had ever been
governed. Nor were they a people whom it was perfectly 25
safe to attack. Their land was indeed an open plain,
destitute of natural defences; but their veins were full of the
high blood of Afghanistan. As soldiers, they had not the
steadiness which is seldom found except in company with
strict discipline; but their impetuous valour had been proved 30
on many fields of battle. It was said that their chiefs, when
united by common peril, could bring eighty thousand men
into the field. Sujah Dowlah had himself seen them fight,

and wisely shrank from a conflict with them. There was in
India one army, and only one, against which even those
proud Caucasian tribes could not stand. It had been
abundantly proved that neither tenfold odds, nor the martial
5 ardour of the boldest Asiatic nations, could avail aught
against English science and resolution. Was it possible to
induce the Governor of Bengal to let out to hire the
irresistible energies of the imperial people, the skill against
which the ablest chiefs of Hindostan were helpless as infants,
10 the discipline which had so often triumphed over the frantic
struggles of fanaticism and despair, the unconquerable
British courage which is never so sedate and stubborn as
towards the close of a doubtful and murderous day?

This was what the Nabob Vizier asked, and what
15 Hastings granted. A bargain was soon struck. Each of
the negotiators had what the other wanted. Hastings was
in need of funds to carry on the government of Bengal, and
to send remittances to London; and Sujah Dowlah had an
ample revenue. Sujah Dowlah was bent on subjugating the
20 Rohillas; and Hastings had at his disposal the only force
by which the Rohillas could be subjugated. It was agreed
that an English army should be lent to the Nabob Vizier,
and that, for the loan, he should pay four hundred thousand
pounds sterling, besides defraying all the charge of the
25 troops while employed in his service.

"I really cannot see," says the Reverend Mr Gleig,
"upon what grounds, either of political or moral justice, this
proposition deserves to be stigmatized as infamous." If we
understand the meaning of words, it is infamous to commit
30 a wicked action for hire, and it is wicked to engage in war
without provocation. In this particular war, scarcely one
aggravating circumstance was wanting. The object of the
Rohilla war was this, to deprive a large population, who had

never done us the least harm, of a good government, and to
place them, against their will, under an execrably bad one.
Nay, even this is not all. England now descended far below
the level even of those petty German princes who, about the
same time, sold us troops to fight the Americans. The 5
hussar-mongers of Hesse and Anspach had at least the
assurance that the expeditions on which their soldiers were
to be employed would be conducted in conformity with the
humane rules of civilised warfare. Was the Rohilla war
likely to be so conducted? Did the Governor stipulate that 10
it should be so conducted? He well knew what Indian
warfare was. He well knew that the power which he
covenanted to put into Sujah Dowlah's hands would, in all
probability, be atrociously abused; and he required no
guarantee, no promise that it should not be so abused. He 15
did not even reserve to himself the right of withdrawing his
aid in case of abuse, however gross. Mr Gleig repeats
Major Scott's absurd plea, that Hastings was justified in
letting out English troops to slaughter the Rohillas, because
the Rohillas were not of Indian race, but a colony from a 20
distant country. What were the English themselves? Was
it for them to proclaim a crusade for the expulsion of all
intruders from the countries watered by the Ganges? Did
it lie in their mouths to contend that a foreign settler who
establishes an empire in India is a *caput lupinum?* What 25
would they have said if any other power had, on such a
ground, attacked Madras or Calcutta, without the slightest
provocation? Such a defence was wanting to make the
infamy of the transaction complete. The atrocity of the
crime, and the hypocrisy of the apology, are worthy of each 30
other.

One of the three brigades of which the Bengal army
consisted was sent under Colonel Champion to join Sujah

Dowlah's forces.   The Rohillas expostulated, entreated,
offered a large ransom, but in vain.   They then resolved
to defend themselves to the last.   A bloody battle was
fought.   "The enemy," says Colonel Champion, "gave proof
5 of a good share of military knowledge; and it is impossible
to describe a more obstinate firmness of resolution than they
displayed."   The dastardly sovereign of Oude fled from the
field.   The English were left unsupported; but their fire
and their charge were irresistible.   It was not, however, till
10 the most distinguished chiefs had fallen, fighting bravely at
the head of their troops, that the Rohilla ranks gave way.
Then the Nabob Vizier and his rabble made their appearance, and hastened to plunder the camp of the valiant
enemies, whom they had never dared to look in the face.
15 The soldiers of the Company, trained in an exact discipline,
kept unbroken order, while the tents were pillaged by these
worthless allies.   But many voices were heard to exclaim,
"We have had all the fighting, and those rogues are to have
all the profit."
20   Then the horrors of Indian war were let loose on the fair
valleys and cities of Rohilcund.   The whole country was in
a blaze.   More than a hundred thousand people fled from
their homes to pestilential jungles, preferring famine, and
fever, and the haunts of tigers, to the tyranny of him, to
25 whom an English and a Christian government had, for
shameful lucre, sold their substance, and their blood, and
the honour of their wives and daughters.   Colonel Champion
remonstrated with the Nabob Vizier, and sent strong representations to Fort William ; but the Governor had made no
30 conditions as to the mode in which the war was to be carried
on.   He had troubled himself about nothing but his forty
lacs ; and, though he might disapprove of Sujah Dowlah's
wanton barbarity, he did not think himself entitled to inter-

fere, except by offering advice. This delicacy excites the
admiration of the reverend biographer. "Mr Hastings,"
he says, "could not himself dictate to the Nabob, nor permit
the commander of the Company's troops to dictate how the
war was to be carried on." No, to be sure. Mr Hastings 5
had only to put down by main force the brave struggles of
innocent men fighting for their liberty. Their military
resistance crushed, his duties ended; and he had then only
to fold his arms and look on, while their villages were
burned, their children butchered, and their women violated. 10
Will Mr Gleig seriously maintain this opinion? Is any
rule more plain than this, that whoever voluntarily gives to
another irresistible power over human beings, is bound to
take order that such power shall not be barbarously abused?
But we beg pardon of our readers for arguing a point so 15
clear.

We hasten to the end of this sad and disgraceful story.
The war ceased. The finest population in India was subjected to a greedy, cowardly, cruel tyrant. Commerce and
agriculture languished. The rich province which had 20
tempted the cupidity of Sujah Dowlah became the most
miserable part even of his miserable dominions. Yet is the
injured nation not extinct. At long intervals gleams of its
ancient spirit have flashed forth; and even at this day,
valour, and self-respect, and a chivalrous feeling rare among 25
Asiatics, and a bitter remembrance of the great crime of
England, distinguish that noble Afghan race. To this day
they are regarded as the best of all sepoys at the cold
steel; and it was very recently remarked, by one who had
enjoyed great opportunities of observation, that the only 30
natives of India to whom the word "gentleman" can with
perfect propriety be applied are to be found among the
Rohillas.

Whatever we may think of the morality of Hastings, it cannot be denied that the financial results of his policy did honour to his talents. In less than two years after he assumed the government, he had, without imposing any 5 additional burdens on the people subject to his authority, added about four hundred and fifty thousand pounds to the annual income of the Company, besides procuring about a million in ready money. He had also relieved the finances of Bengal from military expenditure, amounting to near a 10 quarter of a million a year, and had thrown that charge on the Nabob of Oude. There can be no doubt that this was a result which, if it had been obtained by honest means, would have entitled him to the warmest gratitude of his country, and which, by whatever means obtained, proved that he 15 possessed great talents for administration.

In the mean time, Parliament had been engaged in long and grave discussions on Asiatic affairs. The ministry of Lord North, in the session of 1773, introduced a measure which made a considerable change in the constitution of the 20 Indian government. This law, known by the name of the Regulating Act, provided that the presidency of Bengal should exercise a control over the other possessions of the Company; that the chief of that presidency should be styled Governor-General; that he should be assisted by four Coun- 25 cillors; and that a supreme court of judicature, consisting of a chief justice and three inferior judges, should be established at Calcutta. This court was made independent of the Governor-General and Council, and was intrusted with a civil and criminal jurisdiction of immense, and, at the same 30 time, of undefined extent.

The Governor-General and Councillors were named in the Act, and were to hold their situations for five years. Hastings was to be the first Governor-General. One of the four new Councillors, Mr Barwell, an experienced servant of the Company, was then in India. The other three, General Clavering, Mr Monson, and Mr Francis, were sent out from England.

The ablest of the new Councillors was, beyond all doubt, 5 Philip Francis. His acknowledged compositions prove that he possessed considerable eloquence and information. Several years passed in the public offices had formed him to habits of business. His enemies have never denied that he had a fearless and manly spirit; and his friends, we are 10 afraid, must acknowledge that his estimate of himself was extravagantly high, that his temper was irritable, that his deportment was often rude and petulant, and that his hatred was of intense bitterness and of long duration.

It is scarcely possible to mention this eminent man with- 15 out adverting for a moment to the question which his name at once suggests to every mind. Was he the author of the Letters of Junius? Our own firm belief is that he was. The evidence is, we think, such as would support a verdict in a civil, nay, in a criminal proceeding. The handwriting 20 of Junius is the very peculiar handwriting of Francis, slightly disguised. As to the position, pursuits, and connections of Junius, the following are the most important facts which can be considered as clearly proved: first, that he was acquainted with the technical forms of the secretary 25 of state's office; secondly, that he was intimately acquainted with the business of the war-office; thirdly, that he, during the year 1770, attended debates in the House of Lords, and took notes of speeches, particularly of the speeches of Lord Chatham; fourthly, that he bitterly resented the appoint- 30 ment of Mr Chamier to the place of deputy secretary-at-war; fifthly, that he was bound by some strong tie to the first Lord Holland. Now, Francis passed some years in the

secretary of state's office. He was subsequently chief clerk
of the war-office. He repeatedly mentioned that he had
himself, in 1770, heard speeches of Lord Chatham ; and
some of these speeches were actually printed from his notes.
5 He resigned his clerkship at the war-office from resentment
at the appointment of Mr Chamier. It was by Lord
Holland that he was first introduced into the public service.
Now, here are five marks, all of which ought to be found in
Junius. They are all five found in Francis. We do not
10 believe that more than two of them can be found in any
other person whatever. If this argument does not settle the
question, there is an end of all reasoning on circumstantial
evidence.

The internal evidence seems to us to point the same
15 way. The style of Francis bears a strong resemblance to
that of Junius ; nor are we disposed to admit, what is
generally. taken for granted, that the acknowledged compositions of Francis are very decidedly inferior to the
anonymous letters. The argument from inferiority, at all
20 events, is one which may be urged with at least equal force
against every claimant that has ever been mentioned, with
the single exception of Burke ; and it would be a waste of
time to prove that Burke was not Junius. And what
conclusion, after all, can be drawn from mere inferiority ?
25 Every writer must produce his best work ; and the interval
between his best work and his second best work may be
very wide indeed. Nobody will say that the best letters of
Junius are more decidedly superior to the acknowledged
works of Francis than three or four of Corneille's tragedies
30 to the rest, than three or four of Ben Jonson's comedies to
the rest, than the Pilgrim's Progress to the other works of
Bunyan, than Don Quixote to the other works of Cervantes.
Nay, it is certain that the Man in the Mask, whoever he

may have been, was a most unequal writer. To go no
further than the letters which bear the signature of Junius;
the letter to the king, and the letters to Horne Tooke, have
little in common, except the asperity; and asperity was an
ingredient seldom wanting either in the writings or in the 5
speeches of Francis.

Indeed one of the strongest reasons for believing that
Francis was Junius is the moral resemblance between the
two men. It is not difficult, from the letters which, under
various signatures, are known to have been written by 10
Junius, and from his dealings with Woodfall and others, to
form a tolerably correct notion of his character. He was
clearly a man not destitute of real patriotism and magnanimity, a man whose vices were not of a sordid kind. But
he must also have been a man in the highest degree arrogant 15
and insolent, a man prone to malevolence, and prone to the
error of mistaking his malevolence for public virtue. " Doest
thou well to be angry?" was the question asked in old time
of the Hebrew prophet. And he answered, "I do well."
This was evidently the temper of Junius; and to this cause 20
we attribute the savage cruelty which disgraces several of
his letters. No man is so merciless as he who, under a
strong self-delusion, confounds his antipathies with his
duties. It may be added that Junius, though allied with
the democratic party by common enmities, was the very 25
opposite of a democratic politician. While attacking individuals with a ferocity which perpetually violated all the
laws of literary warfare, he regarded the most defective parts
of old institutions with a respect amounting to pedantry,
pleaded the cause of Old Sarum with fervour, and con- 30
temptuously told the capitalists of Manchester and Leeds
that, if they wanted votes, they might buy land and become
freeholders of Lancashire and Yorkshire. All this, we

believe, might stand, with scarcely any change, for a
character of Philip Francis.

It is not strange that the great anonymous writer should
have been willing at that time to leave the country which
5 had been so powerfully stirred by his eloquence. Every
thing had gone against him. That party which he clearly
preferred to every other, the party of George Grenville, had
been scattered by the death of its chief; and Lord Suffolk
had led the greater part of it over to the ministerial benches.
10 The ferment produced by the Middlesex election had gone
down. Every faction must have been alike an object of
aversion to Junius. His opinions on domestic affairs separated him from the ministry; his opinions on colonial affairs
from the opposition. Under such circumstances, he had
15 thrown down his pen in misanthropical despair. His fare-
well letter to Woodfall bears date the nineteenth of January,
1773. In that letter, he declared that he must be an idiot
to write again; that he had meant well by the cause and the
public; that both were given up; that there were not ten
20 men who would act steadily together on any question. "But
it is all alike," he added, "vile and contemptible. You have
never flinched that I know of; and I shall always rejoice to
hear of your prosperity." These were the last words of
Junius. In a year from that time, Philip Francis was on
25 his voyage to Bengal.

With the three new Councillors came out the judges of
the Supreme Court. The chief justice was Sir Elijah Impey.
He was an old acquaintance of Hastings; and it is probable
that the Governor-General, if he had searched through all
30 the inns of court, could not have found an equally serviceable tool. But the members of Council were by no means
in an obsequious mood. Hastings greatly disliked the new
form of government, and had no very high opinion of his

coadjutors. They had heard of this, and were disposed to be suspicious and punctilious. When men are in such a frame of mind, any trifle is sufficient to give occasion for dispute. The members of Council expected a salute of twenty-one guns from the batteries of Fort William. Hastings 5 allowed them only seventeen. They landed in ill-humour. The first civilities were exchanged with cold reserve. On the morrow commenced that long quarrel which, after distracting British India, was renewed in England, and in which all the most eminent statesmen and orators of the age took 10 active part on one or the other side.

Hastings was supported by Barwell. They had not always been friends. But the arrival of the new members of Council from England naturally had the effect of uniting the old servants of the Company. Clavering, Monson, and 15 Francis formed the majority. They instantly wrested the government out of the hands of Hastings; condemned, certainly not without justice, his late dealings with the Nabob Vizier; recalled the English agent from Oude, and sent thither a creature of their own; ordered the brigade 20 which had conquered the unhappy Rohillas to return to the Company's territories; and instituted a severe inquiry into the conduct of the war. Next, in spite of the Governor-General's remonstrances, they proceeded to exercise, in the most indiscreet manner, their new authority over the sub- 25 ordinate presidencies; threw all the affairs of Bombay into confusion; and interfered, with an incredible union of rashness and feebleness, in the intestine disputes of the Mahratta government. At the same time, they fell on the internal administration of Bengal, and attacked the whole fiscal and 30 judicial system, a system which was undoubtedly defective, but which it was very improbable that gentlemen fresh from England would be competent to amend. The effect of their

reforms was that all protection to life and property was
withdrawn, and that gangs of robbers plundered and
slaughtered with impunity in the very suburbs of Calcutta.
Hastings continued to live in the Government-house, and to
5 draw the salary of Governor-General. He continued even
to take the lead at the council-board in the transaction of
ordinary business ; for his opponents could not but feel that
he knew much of which they were ignorant, and that he
decided, both surely and speedily, many questions which to
10 them would have been hopelessly puzzling. But the higher
powers of government and the most valuable patronage had
been taken from him.

The natives soon found this out. They considered him
as a fallen man ; and they acted after their kind. Some of
15 our readers may have seen, in India, a cloud of crows
pecking a sick vulture to death, no bad type of what
happens in that country, as often as fortune deserts one who
has been great and dreaded. In an instant, all the syco-
phants who had lately been ready to lie for him, to forge
20 for him, to pander for him, to poison for him, hasten to
purchase the favour of his victorious enemies by accusing
him. An Indian government has only to let it be understood that it wishes a particular man to be ruined ; and, in
twenty-four hours, it will be furnished with grave charges,
25 supported by depositions so full and circumstantial that any
person unaccustomed to Asiatic mendacity would regard
them as decisive. It is well if the signature of the destined
victim is not counterfeited at the foot of some illegal compact, and if some treasonable paper is not slipped into a
30 hiding-place in his house. Hastings was now regarded as
helpless. The power to make or mar the fortune of every
man in Bengal had passed, as it seemed, into the hands of
the new Councillors. Immediately charges against the

WARREN HASTINGS.   41

Governor-General began to pour in. They were eagerly
welcomed by the majority, who, to do them justice, were
men of too much honour knowingly to countenance false
accusations, but who were not sufficiently acquainted with
the East to be aware that, in that part of the world, a very 5
little encouragement from power will call forth, in a week,
more Oateses, and Bedloes, and Dangerfields, than Westminster Hall sees in a century.

It would have been strange indeed if, at such a juncture,
Nuncomar had remained quiet. That bad man was stimu- 10
lated at once by malignity, by avarice, and by ambition.
Now was the time to be avenged on his old enemy, to wreak
a grudge of seventeen years, to establish himself in the
favour of the majority of the Council, to become the greatest
native in Bengal. From the time of the arrival of the new 15
Councillors, he had paid the most marked court to them,
and had in consequence been excluded, with all indignity,
from the Government-house. He now put into the hands
of Francis, with great ceremony, a paper containing several
charges of the most serious description. By this document 20
Hastings was accused of putting offices up to sale, and of
receiving bribes for suffering offenders to escape. In particular, it was alleged that Mahommed Reza Khan had been
dismissed with impunity, in consideration of a great sum
paid to the Governor-General.   25

Francis read the paper in Council. A violent altercation
followed. Hastings complained in bitter terms of the way
in which he was treated, spoke with contempt of Nuncomar
and of Nuncomar's accusation, and denied the right of the
Council to sit in judgment on the Governor. At the next 30
meeting of the Board, another communication from Nuncomar was produced. He requested that he might be
permitted to attend the Council, and that he might be heard

in support of his assertions. Another tempestuous debate
took place. The Governor-General maintained that the
council-room was not a proper place for such an investigation ; that from persons who were heated by daily conflict
5 with him he could not expect the fairness of judges ; and
that he could not, without betraying the dignity of his post,
submit to be confronted with such a man as Nuncomar.
The majority, however, resolved to go into the charges.
Hastings rose, declared the sitting at an end, and left the
10 room followed by Barwell.   The other members kept their
seats, voted themselves a council, put Clavering in the chair,
and ordered Nuncomar to be called in.   Nuncomar not
only adhered to the original charges, but, after the fashion
of the East, produced a large supplement.   He stated that
15 Hastings had received a great sum for appointing Rajah
Goordas treasurer of the Nabob's household, and for com-
mitting the care of his Highness's person to the Munny
Begum.   He put in a letter purporting to bear the seal of
the Munny Begum, for the purpose of establishing the truth
20 of his story.   The seal, whether forged, as Hastings affirmed,
or genuine, as we are rather inclined to believe, proved
nothing.   Nuncomar, as every body knows who knows India,
had only to tell the Munny Begum that such a letter would
give pleasure to the majority of the Council, in order to
25 procure her attestation.   The majority, however, voted that
the charge was made out; that Hastings had corruptly
received between thirty and forty thousand pounds ; and
that he ought to be compelled to refund.

    The general feeling among the English in Bengal was
30 strongly in favour of the Governor-General.   In talents for
business, in knowledge of the country, in general courtesy
of demeanour, he was decidedly superior to his persecutors.
The servants of the Company were naturally disposed to

side with the most distinguished member of their own body against a clerk from the war-office, who, profoundly ignorant of the native languages and the native character, took on himself to regulate every department of the administration. Hastings, however, in spite of the general sympathy of his 5 countrymen, was in a most painful situation. There was still an appeal to higher authority in England. If that authority took part with his enemies, nothing was left to him but to throw up his office. He accordingly placed his resignation in the hands of his agent in London, Colonel 10 Macleane. But Macleane was instructed not to produce the resignation, unless it should be fully ascertained that the feeling at the India House was adverse to the Governor-General.

The triumph of Nuncomar seemed to be complete. He 15 held a daily levee, to which his countrymen resorted in crowds, and to which, on one occasion, the majority of the Council condescended to repair. His house was an office for the purpose of receiving charges against the Governor-General. It was said that, partly by threats, and partly by 20 wheedling, the villanous Brahmin had induced many of the wealthiest men of the province to send in complaints. But he was playing a perilous game. It was not safe to drive to despair a man of such resources and of such determination as Hastings. Nuncomar, with all his acuteness, did not 25 understand the nature of the institutions under which he lived. He saw that he had with him the majority of the body which made treaties, gave places, raised taxes. The separation between political and judicial functions was a thing of which he had no conception. It had probably 30 never occurred to him that there was in Bengal an authority perfectly independent of the Council, an authority which could protect one whom the Council wished to destroy, and

send to the gibbet one whom the Council wished to protect.
Yet such was the fact. The Supreme Court was, within the
sphere of its own duties, altogether independent of the
Government. Hastings, with his usual sagacity, had seen
5 how much advantage he might derive from possessing himself of this stronghold; and he had acted accordingly. The
Judges, especially the Chief Justice, were hostile to the
majority of the Council. The time had now come for
putting this formidable machinery into action.

10   On a sudden, Calcutta was astounded by the news that
Nuncomar had been taken up on a charge of felony, committed, and thrown into the common gaol. The crime
imputed to him was that six years before he had forged a
bond. The ostensible prosecutor was a native. But it was
15 then, and still is, the opinion of every body, idiots and
biographers excepted, that Hastings was the real mover in
the business.

The rage of the majority rose to the highest point. They
protested against the proceedings of the Supreme Court, and
20 sent several urgent messages to the Judges, demanding that
Nuncomar should be admitted to bail. The Judges returned
haughty and resolute answers. All that the Council could
do was to heap honours and emoluments on the family of
Nuncomar; and this they did. In the mean time the assizes
25 commenced; a true bill was found; and Nuncomar was
brought before Sir Elijah Impey and a jury composed of
Englishmen. A great quantity of contradictory swearing,
and the necessity of having every word of the evidence
interpreted, protracted the trial to a most unusual length.
30 At last a verdict of guilty was returned, and the Chief
Justice pronounced sentence of death on the prisoner.

Mr Gleig is so strangely ignorant as to imagine that the
Judges had no further discretion in the case, and that the

power of extending mercy to Nuncomar resided with the Council. He therefore throws on Francis and Francis's party the whole blame of what followed. We should have thought that a gentleman who has published five or six bulky volumes on Indian affairs might have taken the 5 trouble to inform himself as to the fundamental principles of the Indian Government. The Supreme Court had, under the Regulating Act, the power to respite criminals till the pleasure of the Crown should be known. The Council had, at that time, no power to interfere. 10

That Impey ought to have respited Nuncomar we hold to be perfectly clear. Whether the whole proceeding was not illegal, is a question. But it is certain that, whatever may have been, according to technical rules of construction, the effect of the statute under which the trial took place, it 15 was most unjust to hang a Hindoo for forgery. The law which made forgery capital in England was passed without the smallest reference to the state of society in India. It was unknown to the natives of India. It had never been put in execution among them, certainly not for want of de- 20 linquents. It was in the highest degree shocking to all their notions. They were not accustomed to the distinction which many circumstances, peculiar to our own state of society, have led us to make between forgery and other kinds of cheating. The counterfeiting of a seal was, in 25 their estimation, a common act of swindling; nor had it ever crossed their minds that it was to be punished as severely as gang-robbery or assassination. A just judge would, beyond all doubt, have reserved the case for the consideration of the sovereign. But Impey would not hear 30 of mercy or delay.

The excitement among all classes was great. Francis and Francis's few English adherents described the Governor-

General and the Chief Justice as the worst of murderers.
Clavering, it was said, swore that, even at the foot of the
gallows, Nuncomar should be rescued. The bulk of the
European society, though strongly attached to the Governor-
5 General, could not but feel compassion for a man who, with
all his crimes, had so long filled so large a space in their
sight, who had been great and powerful before the British
empire in India began to exist, and to whom, in the old
times, governors and members of council, then mere com-
10 mercial factors, had paid court for protection. The feeling
of the Hindoos was infinitely stronger. They were, indeed,
not a people to strike one blow for their countryman. But
his sentence filled them with sorrow and dismay. Tried
even by their low standard of morality, he was a bad man.
15 But, bad as he was, he was the head of their race and
religion, a Brahmin of the Brahmins. He had inherited
the purest and highest caste. He had practised with the
greatest punctuality all those ceremonies to which the superstitious Bengalees ascribe far more importance than to the
20 correct discharge of the social duties. They felt, therefore,
as a devout Catholic in the dark ages would have felt, at
seeing a prelate of the highest dignity sent to the gallows by
a secular tribunal. According to their old national laws, a
Brahmin could not be put to death for any crime whatever.
25 And the crime for which Nuncomar was about to die was
regarded by them in much the same light in which the
selling of an unsound horse, for a sound price, is regarded
by a Yorkshire jockey.

The Mussulmans alone appear to have seen with exulta-
30 tion the fate of the powerful Hindoo, who had attempted to
rise by means of the ruin of Mahommed Reza Khan. The
Mahommedan historian of those times takes delight in
aggravating the charge. He assures us that in Nuncomar's

house a casket was found containing counterfeits of the seals
of all the richest men of the province. We have never fallen
in with any other authority for this story, which in itself is
by no means improbable.

The day drew near; and Nuncomar prepared himself to 5
die with that quiet fortitude with which the Bengalee, so
effeminately timid in personal conflict, often encounters
calamities for which there is no remedy. The sheriff, with
the humanity which is seldom wanting in an English gentleman, visited the prisoner on the eve of the execution, and 10
assured him that no indulgence, consistent with the law,
should be réfused to him. Nuncomar expressed his gratitude with great politeness and unaltered composure. Not
a muscle of his face moved. Not a sigh broke from him.
He put his finger to his forehead, and calmly said that fate 15
would have its way, and that there was no resisting the
pleasure of God. He sent his compliments to Francis,
Clavering, and Monson, and charged them to protect Rajah
Goordas, who was about to become the head of the Brahmins of Bengal. The sheriff withdrew, greatly agitated by 20
what had passed, and Nuncomar sat composedly down to
write notes and examine accounts.

The next morning, before the sun was in his power, an
immense concourse assembled round the place where the
gallows had been set up. Grief and horror were on every 25
face; yet to the last the multitude could hardly believe that
the English really purposed to take the life of the great
Brahmin. At length the mournful procession came through
the crowd. Nuncomar sat up in his palanquin, and looked
round him with unaltered serenity. He had just parted 30
from those who were most nearly connected with him.
Their cries and contortions had appalled the European
ministers of justice, but had not produced the smallest

effect on the iron stoicism of the prisoner. The only anxiety
which he expressed was that men of his own priestly caste
might be in attendance to take charge of his corpse. He
again desired to be remembered to his friends in the Council,
5 mounted the scaffold with firmness, and gave the signal to
the executioner. The moment that the drop fell, a howl of
sorrow and despair rose from the innumerable spectators.
Hundreds turned away their faces from the polluting sight,
fled with loud wailings towards the Hoogley, and plunged
10 into its holy waters, as if to purify themselves from the guilt
of having looked on such a crime. These feelings were not
confined to Calcutta. The whole province was greatly excited; and the population of Dacca, in particular, gave
strong signs of grief and dismay.

15   Of Impey's conduct it is impossible to speak too severely.
We have already said that, in our opinion, he acted unjustly
in refusing to respite Nuncomar. No rational man can doubt
that he took this course in order to gratify the Governor-
General. If we had ever had any doubts on that point, they
20 would have been dispelled by a letter which Mr Gleig has
published. Hastings, three or four years later, described
Impey as the man " to whose support he was at one time
indebted for the safety of his fortune, honour, and reputation." These strong words can refer only to the case of
25 Nuncomar; and they must mean that Impey hanged Nuncomar in order to support Hastings. It is, therefore, our
deliberate opinion that Impey, sitting as a judge, put a man
unjustly to death in order to serve a political purpose.

But we look on the conduct of Hastings in a somewhat
30 different light. He was struggling for fortune, honour,
liberty, all that makes life valuable. He was beset by
rancorous and unprincipled enemies. From his colleagues
he could expect no justice. He cannot be blamed for wish-

ing to crush his accusers. He was indeed bound to use only
legitimate means for that end. But it was not strange that
he should have thought any means legitimate which were
pronounced legitimate by the sages of the law, by men whose
peculiar duty it was to deal justly between adversaries, and 5
whose education might be supposed to have peculiarly quali-
fied them for the discharge of that duty. Nobody demands
from a party the unbending equity of a judge. The reason
that judges are appointed is, that even a good man cannot be
trusted to decide a cause in which he is himself concerned. 10
Not a day passes on which an honest prosecutor does not
ask for what none but a dishonest tribunal would grant. It
is too much to expect that any man, when his dearest
interests are at stake, and his strongest passions excited,
will, as against himself, be more just than the sworn 15
dispensers of justice. To take an analogous case from the
history of our own island : suppose that Lord Stafford, when
in the Tower on suspicion of being concerned in the Popish
plot, had been apprised that Titus Oates had done something which might, by a questionable construction, be 20
brought under the head of felony. Should we severely
blame Lord Stafford, in the supposed case, for causing a
prosecution to be instituted, for furnishing funds, for using
all his influence to intercept the mercy of the Crown? We
think not. If a judge, indeed, from favour to the Catholic 25
lords, were to strain the law in order to hang Oates, such a
judge would richly deserve impeachment. But it does not
appear to us that the Catholic lord, by bringing the case
before the judge for decision, would materially overstep the
limits of a just self-defence. 30

While, therefore, we have not the least doubt that this
memorable execution is to be attributed to Hastings, we
doubt whether it can with justice be reckoned among his

crimes. That his conduct was dictated by a profound policy
is evident. He was in a minority in Council. It was possible
that he might long be in a minority. He knew the native
character well. He knew in what abundance accusations are
5 certain to flow in against the most innocent inhabitant of
India who is under the frown of power. There was not in
the whole black population of Bengal a place-holder, a place-
hunter, a government tenant, who did not think that he
might better himself by sending up a deposition against the
10 Governor-General. Under these circumstances, the persecuted statesman resolved to teach the whole crew of accusers
and witnesses that, though in a minority at the council board,
he was still to be feared. The lesson which he gave them
was indeed a lesson not to be forgotten. The head of the
15 combination which had been formed against him, the richest,
the most powerful, the most artful of the Hindoos, distinguished by the favour of those who then held the government,
fenced round by the superstitious reverence of millions, was
hanged in broad day before many thousands of people.
20 Every thing that could make the warning impressive, dignity
in the sufferer, solemnity in the proceeding, was found in
this case. The helpless rage and vain struggles of the
Council made the triumph more signal. From that moment
the conviction of every native was that it was safer to take
25 the part of Hastings in a minority than that of Francis in a
majority, and that he who was so venturous as to join in
running down the Governor-General might chance, in the
phrase of the Eastern poet, to find a tiger, while beating the
jungle for a deer. The voices of a thousand informers were
30 silenced in an instant. From that time, whatever difficulties
Hastings might have to encounter, he was never molested
by accusations from natives of India.

It is a remarkable circumstance that one of the letters of

Hastings to Dr Johnson bears date a very few hours after
the death of Nuncomar. While the whole settlement was in
commotion, while a mighty and ancient priesthood were
weeping over the remains of their chief, the conqueror in
that deadly grapple sat down, with characteristic self-posses- 5
sion, to write about the Tour to the Hebrides, Jones's Persian
Grammar, and the history, traditions, arts, and natural productions of India.

In the mean time, intelligence of the Rohilla war, and of
the first disputes between Hastings and his colleagues, had 10
reached London. The directors took part with the majority,
and sent out a letter filled with severe reflections on the conduct of Hastings. They condemned, in strong but just terms,
the iniquity of undertaking offensive wars merely for the
sake of pecuniary advantages. But they utterly forgot that, 15
if Hastings had by illicit means obtained pecuniary advantages, he had done so, not for his own benefit, but in order
to meet their demands. To enjoin honesty, and to insist on
having what could not be honestly got, was then the constant
practice of the Company. As Lady Macbeth says of her 20
husband, they "would not play false, and yet would wrongly
win."

The Regulating Act, by which Hastings had been appointed Governor-General for five years, empowered the
Crown to remove him on an address from the Company. 25
Lord North was desirous to procure such an address. The
three members of Council who had been sent out from
England were men of his own choice. General Clavering, in
particular, was supported by a large parliamentary connection, such as no cabinet could be inclined to disoblige. The 30
wish of the Minister was to displace Hastings, and to put
Clavering at the head of the government. In the Court of
Directors parties were very nearly balanced. Eleven voted

4—2

against Hastings; ten for him. The Court of Proprietors
was then convened. The great sale-room presented a singular
appearance. Letters had been sent by the Secretary of the
Treasury, exhorting all the supporters of government who
5 held India stock to be in attendance. Lord Sandwich marshalled the friends of the administration with his usual
dexterity and alertness. Fifty peers and privy councillors,
seldom seen so far eastward, were counted in the crowd.
The debate lasted till midnight. The opponents of Hastings
10 had a small superiority on the division; but a ballot was
demanded; and the result was that the Governor-General
triumphed by a majority of above a hundred votes over the
combined efforts of the Directors and the Cabinet. The ministers were greatly exasperated by this defeat. Even Lord
15 North lost his temper, no ordinary occurrence with him, and
threatened to convoke parliament before Christmas, and to
bring in a bill for depriving the Company of all political
power, and for restricting it to its old business of trading in
silks and teas.

20   Colonel Macleane, who through all this conflict had zeal-
ously supported the cause of Hastings, now thought that his
employer was in imminent danger of being turned out,
branded with parliamentary censure, perhaps prosecuted.
The opinion of the crown lawyers had already been taken
25 respecting some parts of the Governor-General's conduct.
It seemed to be high time to think of securing an honourable retreat. Under these circumstances, Macleane thought
himself justified in producing the resignation with which he
had been intrusted. The instrument was not in very accurate
30 form; but the Directors were too eager to be scrupulous.
They accepted the resignation, fixed on Mr Wheler, one of
their own body, to succeed Hastings, and sent out orders that
General Clavering, as senior member of Council, should

exercise the functions of Governor-General till Mr Wheler should arrive.

But, while these things were passing in England, a great change had taken place in Bengal. Monson was no more. Only four members of the government were left. Clavering 5 and Francis were on one side, Barwell and the Governor-General on the other; and the Governor-General had the casting vote. Hastings, who had been during two years destitute of all power and patronage, became at once absolute. He instantly proceeded to retaliate on his adversaries. Their 10 measures were reversed: their creatures were displaced. A new valuation of the lands of Bengal, for the purposes of taxation, was ordered; and it was provided that the whole inquiry should be conducted by the Governor-General, and that all the letters relating to it should run in his name. He 15 began, at the same time, to revolve vast plans of conquest and dominion, plans which he lived to see realised, though not by himself. His project was to form subsidiary alliances with the native princes, particularly with those of Oude and Berar, and thus to make Britain the paramount power in 20 India. While he was meditating these great designs, arrived the intelligence that he had ceased to be Governor-General, that his resignation had been accepted, that Wheler was coming out immediately, and that, till Wheler arrived, the chair was to be filled by Clavering. 25

Had Hastings still been in a minority, he would probably have retired without a struggle; but he was now the real master of British India, and he was not disposed to quit his high place. He asserted that he had never given any instructions which could warrant the steps taken at home. 30 What his instructions had been, he owned he had forgotten. If he had kept a copy of them he had mislaid it. But he was certain that he had repeatedly declared to the Directors

that he would not resign. He could not see how the court, possessed of that declaration from himself, could receive his resignation from the doubtful hands of an agent. If the resignation were invalid, all the proceedings which were
5 founded on that resignation were null, and Hastings was still Governor-General.

He afterwards affirmed that, though his agents had not acted in conformity with his instructions, he would nevertheless have held himself bound by their acts, if Clavering
10 had not attempted to seize the supreme power by violence. Whether this assertion were or were not true, it cannot be doubted that the imprudence of Clavering gave Hastings an advantage. The General sent for the keys of the fort and of the treasury, took possession of the records, and held a
15 council at which Francis attended. Hastings took the chair in another apartment, and Barwell sat with him. Each of the two parties had a plausible show of right. There was no authority entitled to their obedience within fifteen thousand miles. It seemed that there remained no way of settling
20 the dispute except an appeal to arms; and from such an appeal Hastings, confident of his influence over his countrymen in India, was not inclined to shrink. He directed the officers of the garrison of Fort William and of all the neighbouring stations to obey no ·orders but his. At the same
25 time, with admirable judgment, he offered to submit the case to the Supreme Court, and to abide by its decision. By making this proposition he risked nothing; yet it was a proposition which his opponents could hardly reject. Nobody could be treated as a criminal for obeying what the
30 judges should solemnly pronounce to be the lawful government. The boldest man would shrink from taking arms in defence of what the judges should pronounce to be usurpation. Clavering and Francis, after some delay, unwillingly

consented to abide by the award of the court. The court pronounced that the resignation was invalid, and that therefore Hastings was still Governor-General under the Regulating Act ; and the defeated members of the Council, finding that the sense of the whole settlement was against 5 them, acquiesced in the decision.

About this time arrived the news that, after a suit which had lasted several years, the Franconian courts had decreed a divorce between Imhoff and his wife. The Baron left Calcutta, carrying with him the means of buying an 10 estate in Saxony. The lady became Mrs Hastings. The event was celebrated by great festivities ; and all the most conspicuous persons at Calcutta, without distinction of parties, were invited to the Government-house. Clavering, as the Mahommedan chronicler tells the story, was sick 15 in mind and body, and excused himself from joining the splendid assembly. But Hastings, whom, as it should seem, success in ambition and in love had put into high good-humour, would take no denial. He went himself to the General's house, and at length brought his vanquished rival 20 in triumph to the gay circle which surrounded the bride. The exertion was too much for a frame broken by mortification as well as by disease. Clavering died a few days later.

Wheler, who came out expecting to be Governor-General, and was forced to content himself with a seat at the Council 25 Board, generally voted with Francis. But the Governor-General, with Barwell's help and his own casting vote, was still the master. Some change took place at this time in the feeling both of the Court of Directors and of the Ministers of the Crown. All designs against Hastings were 30 dropped ; and when his original term of five years expired, he was quietly re-appointed. The truth is, that the fearful dangers to which the public interests in every quarter were now exposed, made both Lord North and the Company unwilling to part with a Governor whose talents, experience, and resolution, enmity itself was compelled to acknowledge.

The crisis was indeed formidable. That great and 5 victorious empire, on the throne of which George the Third had taken his seat eighteen years before, with brighter hopes than had attended the accession of any of the long line of English sovereigns, had, by the most senseless misgovernment, been brought to the verge of ruin. In America 10 millions of Englishmen were at war with the country from which their blood, their language, their religion, and their institutions were derived, and to which, but a short time before, they had been as strongly attached as the inhabitants of Norfolk and Leicestershire. The great powers of Europe, 15 humbled to the dust by the vigour and genius which had guided the councils of George the Second, now rejoiced in the prospect of a signal revenge. The time was approaching when our island, while struggling to keep down the United States of America, and pressed with a still nearer danger by 20 the too just discontents of Ireland, was to be assailed by France, Spain, and Holland, and to be threatened by the armed neutrality of the Baltic; when even our maritime supremacy was to be in jeopardy; when hostile fleets were to command the Straits of Calpe and the Mexican Sea; 25 when the British flag was to be scarcely able to protect the British Channel. Great as were the faults of Hastings, it was happy for our country that at that conjuncture, the most terrible through which she has ever passed, he was the ruler of her Indian dominions.

30 An attack by sea on Bengal was little to be apprehended. The danger was that the European enemies of England might form an alliance with some native power, might furnish that power with troops, arms, and ammunition, and

might thus assail our possessions on the side of the land. It was chiefly from the Mahrattas that Hastings anticipated danger. The original seat of that singular people was the wild range of hills which runs along the western coast of India. In the reign of Aurungzebe the inhabitants of those 5 regions, led by the great Sevajee, began to descend on the possessions of their wealthier and less warlike neighbours. The energy, ferocity, and cunning of the Mahrattas, soon made them the most conspicuous among the new powers which were generated by the corruption of the decaying 10 monarchy. At first they were only robbers. They soon rose to the dignity of conquerors. Half the provinces of the empire were turned into Mahratta principalities. Freebooters, sprung from low castes, and accustomed to menial employments, became mighty Rajahs. The Bonslas, at the 15 head of a band of plunderers, occupied the vast region of Berar. The Guicowar, which is, being interpreted, the Herdsman, founded that dynasty which still reigns in Guzerat. The houses of Scindia and Holkar waxed great in Malwa. One adventurous captain made his nest on the 20 impregnable rock of Gooti. Another became the lord of the thousand villages which are scattered among the green rice-fields of Tanjore.

That was the time, throughout India, of double government. The form and the power were everywhere separated. 25 The Mussulman nabobs who had become sovereign princes, the Vizier in Oude, and the Nizam at Hyderabad, still called themselves the viceroys of the house of Tamerlane. In the same manner the Mahratta states, though really independent of each other, pretended to be members of one empire. 30 They all acknowledged, by words and ceremonies, the supremacy of the heir of Sevajee, a *roi fainéant* who chewed bang and toyed with dancing girls in a state prison at

Sattara, and of his Peshwa or mayor of the palace, a great
hereditary magistrate, who kept a court with kingly state at
Poonah, and whose authority was obeyed in the spacious
provinces of Aurungabad and Bejapoor.

5   Some months before war was declared in Europe the
government of Bengal was alarmed by the news that a
French adventurer, who passed for a man of quality, had
arrived at Poonah. It was said that he had been received
there with great distinction, that he had delivered to the
10 Peshwa letters and presents from Louis the Sixteenth, and
that a treaty, hostile to England, had been concluded between France and the Mahrattas.

       Hastings immediately resolved to strike the first blow.
The title of the Peshwa was not undisputed.   A portion of
15 the Mahratta nation was favourable to a pretender.   The
Governor-General determined to espouse this pretender's
interest, to move an army across the peninsula of India, and
to form a close alliance with the chief of the house of
Bonsla, who ruled Berar, and who, in power and dignity,
20 was inferior to none of the Mahratta princes.

       The army had marched, and the negotiations with Berar
were in progress, when a letter from the English consul at
Cairo brought the news that war had been proclaimed both
in London and Paris.   All the measures which the crisis
25 required were adopted by Hastings without a moment's
delay.   The French factories in Bengal were seized.   Orders
were sent to Madras that Pondicherry should instantly be
occupied.   Near Calcutta, works were thrown up which were
thought to render the approach of a hostile force impossible.
30 A maritime establishment was formed for the defence of the
river.   Nine new battalions of sepoys were raised, and a
corps of native artillery was formed out of the hardy Lascars
of the Bay of Bengal.   Having made these arrangements,

the Governor-General with calm confidence pronounced his presidency secure from all attack, unless the Mahrattas should march against it in conjunction with the French.

The expedition which Hastings had sent westward was not so speedily or completely successful as most of his 5 undertakings. The commanding officer procrastinated. The authorities at Bombay blundered. But the Governor-General persevered. A new commander repaired the errors of his predecessor. Several brilliant actions spread the military renown of the English through regions where no 10 European flag had ever been seen. It is probable that, if a new and more formidable danger had not compelled Hastings to change his whole policy, his plans respecting the Mahratta empire would have been carried into complete effect. 15

The authorities in England had wisely sent out to Bengal, as commander of the forces and member of the Council, one of the most distinguished soldiers of that time. Sir Eyre Coote had, many years before, been conspicuous among the founders of the British empire in the East. At the council 20 of war which preceded the battle of Plassey, he earnestly recommended, in opposition to the majority, that daring course which, after some hesitation, was adopted, and which was crowned with such splendid success. He subsequently commanded in the south of India against the brave and 25 unfortunate Lally, gained the decisive battle of Wandewash over the French and their native allies, took Pondicherry, and made the English power supreme in the Carnatic. Since those great exploits near twenty years had elapsed. Coote had no longer the bodily activity which he had shown 30 in earlier days; nor was the vigour of his mind altogether unimpaired. He was capricious and fretful, and required much coaxing to keep him in good humour. It must, we

fear, be added that the love of money had grown upon him, and that he thought more about his allowances, and less about his duties, than might have been expected from so eminent a member of so noble a profession. Still he was
5 perhaps the ablest officer that was then to be found in the British army. Among the native soldiers his name was great and his influence unrivalled. Nor is he yet forgotten by them. Now and then a white-bearded old sepoy may still be found, who loves to talk of Porto Novo and Pollilore.
10 It is but a short time since one of those aged men came to present a memorial to an English officer, who holds one of the highest employments in India. A print of Coote hung in the room. The veteran recognised at once that face and figure which he had not seen for more than half a century,
15 and, forgetting his salam to the living, halted, drew himself up, lifted his hand, and with solemn reverence paid his military obeisance to the dead.

Coote, though he did not, like Barwell, vote constantly with the Governor-General, was by no means inclined to
20 join in systematic opposition, and on most questions con-curred with Hastings, who did his best, by assiduous courtship, and by readily granting the most exorbitant allowances, to gratify the strongest passions of the old soldier.

25 It seemed likely at this time that a general reconciliation would put an end to the quarrels which had, during some years, weakened and disgraced the government of Bengal. The dangers of the empire might well induce men of patriotic feeling—and of patriotic feeling neither Hastings
30 nor Francis was destitute—to forget private enmities, and to co-operate heartily for the general good. Coote had never been concerned in faction. Wheler was thoroughly tired of it. Barwell had made an ample fortune, and, though he

had promised that he would not leave Calcutta while his
help was needed in Council, was most desirous to return to
England, and exerted himself to promote an arrangement
which would set him at liberty.   A compact was made, by
which Francis agreed to desist from opposition, and Hastings 5
engaged that the friends of Francis should be admitted to a
fair share of the honours and emoluments of the service.
During a few months after this treaty there was apparent
harmony at the council-board.

Harmony, indeed, was never more necessary; for at this 10
moment internal calamities, more formidable than war itself,
menaced Bengal.   The authors of the Regulating Act of
1773 had established two independent powers, the one
judicial, the other political; and, with a carelessness scanda-
lously common in English legislation, had omitted to define 15
the limits of either.   The judges took advantage of the
indistinctness, and attempted to draw to themselves supreme
authority, not only within Calcutta, but through the whole
of the great territory subject to the presidency of Fort
William.   There are few Englishmen who will not admit 20
that the English law, in spite of modern improvements, is
neither so cheap nor so speedy as might be wished.   Still,
it is a system which has grown up among us.   In some
points, it has been fashioned to suit our feelings; in others,
it has gradually fashioned our feelings to suit itself.   Even 25
to its worst evils we are accustomed; and, therefore, though
we may complain of them, they do not strike us with the
horror and dismay which would be produced by a new
grievance of smaller severity.   In India the case is widely
different.   English law, transplanted to that country, has all 30
the vices from which we suffer here; it has them all in a far
higher degree; and it has other vices, compared with which
the worst vices from which we suffer are trifles.   Dilatory

here, it is far more dilatory in a land where the help of an
interpreter is needed by every judge and by every advocate.
Costly here, it is far more costly in a land into which the
legal practitioners must be imported from an immense
5 distance. All English labour in India, from the labour of
the Governor-General and the Commander-in-Chief, down
to that of a groom or a watchmaker, must be paid for at a
higher rate than at home. No man will be banished, and
banished to the torrid zone, for nothing. The rule holds
10 good with respect to the legal profession. No English
barrister will work, fifteen thousand miles from all his friends,
with the thermometer at ninety-six in the shade, for the
emoluments which will content him in chambers that overlook the Thames. Accordingly, the fees at Calcutta are
15 about three times as great as the fees of Westminster Hall;
and this, though the people of India are, beyond all comparison, poorer than the people of England. Yet the delay
and the expense, grievous as they are, form the smallest
part of the evil which English law, imported without modifi-
20 cations into India, could not fail to produce. The strongest
feelings of our nature, honour, religion, female modesty,
rose up against the innovation. Arrest on mesne process
was the first step in most civil proceedings; and to a native
of rank arrest was not merely a restraint, but a foul personal
25 indignity. Oaths were required in every stage of every suit;
and the feeling of a Quaker about an oath is hardly stronger
than that of a respectable native. That the apartments of a
woman of quality should be entered by strange men, or that
her face should be seen by them, are, in the East, intolerable
30 outrages, outrages which are more dreaded than death, and
which can be expiated only by the shedding of blood. To
these outrages the most distinguished families of Bengal,
Bahar, and Orissa, were now exposed. Imagine what the

state of our own country would be, if a jurisprudence were
on a sudden introduced among us, which should be to us
what our jurisprudence was to our Asiatic subjects.   Imagine
what the state of our country would be, if it were enacted
that any man, by merely swearing that a debt was due to 5
him, should acquire a right to insult the persons of men of
the most honourable and sacred callings and of women of
the most shrinking delicacy, to horsewhip a general officer,
to put a bishop in the stocks, to treat ladies in the way
which called forth the blow of Wat Tyler.   Something like 10
this was the effect of the attempt which the Supreme Court
made to extend its jurisdiction over the whole of the
Company's territory.

A reign of terror began, of terror heightened by mystery;
for even that which was endured was less horrible than that 15
which was anticipated.   No man knew what was next to be
expected from this strange tribunal.   It came from beyond
the black water, as the people of India, with mysterious
horror, call the sea.   It consisted of judges not one of whom
was familiar with the usages of the millions over whom 20
they claimed boundless authority.   Its records were kept
in unknown characters; its sentences were pronounced in
unknown sounds.   It had already collected round itself an
army of the worst part of the native population, informers,
and false witnesses, and common barrators, and agents of 25
chicane, and, above all, a banditti of bailiffs' followers,
compared with whom the retainers of the worst English
spunging-houses, in the worst times, might be considered
as upright and tender-hearted.   Many natives, highly considered among their countrymen, were seized, hurried up to 30
Calcutta, flung into the common gaol, not for any crime
even imputed, not for any debt that had been proved, but
merely as a precaution till their cause should come to trial.

There were instances in which men of the most venerable
dignity, persecuted without a cause by extortioners, died of
rage and shame in the gripe of the vile alguazils of Impey.
The harams of noble Mahommedans, sanctuaries respected
5 in the East, by governments which respected nothing else,
were burst open by gangs of bailiffs. The Mussulmans,
braver and less accustomed to submission than the Hindoos,
sometimes stood on their defence; and there were instances
in which they shed their blood in the doorway, while
10 defending, sword in hand, the sacred apartments of their
women. Nay, it seemed as if even the faint-hearted
Bengalee, who had crouched at the feet of Surajah Dowlah,
who had been mute during the administration of Vansittart,
would at length find courage in despair. No Mahratta
15 invasion had ever spread through the province such dismay
as this inroad of English lawyers. All the injustice of
former oppressors, Asiatic and European, appeared as a
blessing when compared with the justice of the Supreme
Court.

20   Every class of the population, English and native, with
the exception of the ravenous pettifoggers who fattened on
the misery and terror of an immense community, cried out
loudly against this fearful oppression. But the judges were
immovable. If a bailiff was resisted, they ordered the
25 soldiers to be called out. If a servant of the Company, in
conformity with the orders of the government, withstood
the miserable catchpoles who, with Impey's writs in their
hands, exceeded the insolence and rapacity of gang-robbers,
he was flung into prison for a contempt. The lapse of sixty
30 years, the virtue and wisdom of many eminent magistrates
who have during that time administered justice in the
Supreme Court, have not effaced from the minds of the
people of Bengal the recollection of those evil days.

The members of the government were, on this subject, united as one man. Hastings had courted the judges; he had found them useful instruments. But he was not disposed to make them his own masters, or the masters of India. His mind was large; his knowledge of the native character most accurate. He saw that the system pursued by the Supreme Court was degrading to the government and ruinous to the people; and he resolved to oppose it manfully. The consequence was, that the friendship, if that be the proper word for such a connection, which had existed between him and Impey, was for a time completely dissolved. The government placed itself firmly between the tyrannical tribunal and the people. The Chief Justice proceeded to the wildest excesses. The Governor-General and all the members of Council were served with writs, calling on them to appear before the King's justices, and to answer for their public acts. This was too much. Hastings, with just scorn, refused to obey the call, set at liberty the persons wrongfully detained by the Court, and took measures for resisting the outrageous proceedings of the sheriffs' officers, if necessary, by the sword. But he had in view another device which might prevent the necessity of an appeal to arms. He was seldom at a loss for an expedient; and he knew Impey well. The expedient, in this case, was a very simple one, neither more nor less than a bribe. Impey was, by act of parliament, a judge, independent of the government of Bengal, and entitled to a salary of eight thousand a year. Hastings proposed to make him also a judge in the Company's service, removable at the pleasure of the government of Bengal; and to give him, in that capacity, about eight thousand a year more. It was understood that, in consideration of this new salary, Impey would desist from urging the high pretensions of his court. If he did urge

these pretensions, the government could, at a moment's notice, eject him from the new place which had been created for him. The bargain was struck; Bengal was saved; an appeal to force was averted; and the Chief Justice was rich,
5 quiet, and infamous.

Of Impey's conduct it is unnecessary to speak. It was of a piece with almost every part of his conduct that comes under the notice of history. No other such judge has dishonoured the English ermine, since Jefferies drank himself
10 to death in the Tower. But we cannot agree with those who have blamed Hastings for this transaction. The case stood thus. The negligent manner in which the Regulating Act had been framed put it in the power of the Chief Justice to throw a great country into the most dreadful
15 confusion. He was determined to use his power to the utmost, unless he was paid to be still: and Hastings consented to pay him. The necessity was to be deplored. It is also to be deplored that pirates should be able to exact ransom by threatening to make their captives walk the
20 plank. But to ransom a captive from pirates has always been held a humane and Christian act; and it would be absurd to charge the payer of the ransom with corrupting the virtue of the corsair. This, we seriously think, is a not unfair illustration of the relative position of Impey,
25 Hastings, and the people of India. Whether it was right in Impey to demand or to accept a price for powers which, if they really belonged to him, he could not abdicate, which, if they did not belong to him, he ought never to have usurped, and which in neither case he could honestly sell,
30 is one question. It is quite another question, whether Hastings was not right to give any sum, however large, to any man, however worthless, rather than either surrender millions of human beings to pillage, or rescue them by civil war.

Francis strongly opposed this arrangement. It may, indeed, be suspected that personal aversion to Impey was as strong a motive with Francis as regard for the welfare of the province. To a mind burning with resentment, it might seem better to leave Bengal to the oppressors than 5 to redeem it by enriching them. It is not improbable, on the other hand, that Hastings may have been the more willing to resort to an expedient agreeable to the Chief Justice, because that high functionary had already been so serviceable, and might, when existing dissensions were com- 10 posed, be serviceable again.

But it was not on this point alone that Francis was now opposed to Hastings. The peace between them proved to be only a short and hollow truce, during which their mutual aversion was constantly becoming stronger. At length an 15 explosion took place. Hastings publicly charged Francis with having deceived him, and with having induced Barwell to quit the service by insincere promises. Then came a dispute, such as frequently arises even between honourable men, when they may make important agreements by mere verbal 20 communication. An impartial historian will probably be of opinion that they had misunderstood each other; but their minds were so much embittered that they imputed to each other nothing less than deliberate villany. "I do not," said Hastings, in a minute recorded on the Consultations of the 25 Government, "I do not trust to Mr Francis's promises of candour, convinced that he is incapable of it. I judge of his public conduct by his private, which I have found to be void of truth and honour." After the Council had risen, Francis put a challenge into the Governor-General's hand. It was 30 instantly accepted. They met, and fired. Francis was shot through the body. He was carried to a neighbouring house, where it appeared that the wound, though severe, was not

mortal. Hastings inquired repeatedly after his enemy's
health, and proposed to call on him; but Francis coldly
declined the visit. He had a proper sense, he said, of the
Governor-General's politeness, but could not consent to any
5 private interview. They could meet only at the council-
board.

In a very short time it was made signally manifest to how
great a danger the Governor-General had, on this occasion,
exposed his country. A crisis arrived with which he, and he
10 alone, was competent to deal. It is not too much to say that,
if he had been taken from the head of affairs, the years 1780
and 1781 would have been as fatal to our power in Asia as to
our power in America.

The Mahrattas had been the chief objects of apprehension
15 to Hastings. The measures which he had adopted for the
purpose of breaking their power, had at first been frustrated
by the errors of those whom he was compelled to employ;
but his perseverance and ability seemed likely to be crowned
with success, when a far more formidable danger showed
20 itself in a distant quarter.

About thirty years before this time, a Mahommedan
soldier had begun to distinguish himself in the wars of
Southern India. His education had been neglected; his
extraction was humble. His father had been a petty officer
25 of revenue; his grandfather a wandering dervise. But
though thus meanly descended, though ignorant even of
the alphabet, the adventurer had no sooner been placed at
the head of a body of troops than he approved himself a
man born for conquest and command. Among the crowd
30 of chiefs who were struggling for a share of India, none
could compare with him in the qualities of the captain and
the statesman. He became a general; he became a sovereign. Out of the fragments of old principalities, which

had gone to pieces in the general wreck, he formed for
himself a great, compact, and vigorous empire. That empire
he ruled with the ability, severity, and vigilance of Louis
the Eleventh. Licentious in his pleasures, implacable in
his revenge, he had yet enlargement of mind enough to 5
perceive how much the prosperity of subjects adds to the
strength of governments. He was an oppressor; but he
had at least the merit of protecting his people against all
oppression except his own. He was now in extreme old
age; but his intellect was as clear, and his spirit as high, 10
as in the prime of manhood. Such was the great Hyder
Ali, the founder of the Mahommedan kingdom of Mysore,
and the most formidable enemy with whom the English
conquerors of India have ever had to contend.

Had Hastings been governor of Madras, Hyder would 15
have been either made a friend, or vigorously encountered
as an enemy. Unhappily the English authorities in the
south provoked their powerful neighbour's hostility, without
being prepared to repel it. On a sudden, an army of ninety
thousand men, far superior in discipline and efficiency to 20
any other native force that could be found in India, came
pouring through those wild passes which, worn by mountain
torrents, and dark with jungle, lead down from the table-
land of Mysore to the plains of the Carnatic. This great
army was accompanied by a hundred pieces of cannon; and 25
its movements were guided by many French officers, trained
in the best military schools of Europe.

Hyder was everywhere triumphant. The sepoys in
many British garrisons flung down their arms. Some forts
were surrendered by treachery, and some by despair. In a 30
few days the whole open country north of the Coleroon
had submitted. The English inhabitants of Madras could
already see by night, from the top of Mount St Thomas, the

eastern sky reddened by a vast semicircle of blazing villages.
The white villas, to which our countrymen retire after the
daily labours of government and of trade, when the cool
evening breeze springs up from the bay, were now left
5 without inhabitants; for bands of the fierce horsemen of
Mysore had already been seen prowling among the tulip-
trees, and near the gay verandas. Even the town was not
thought secure, and the British merchants and public functionaries made haste to crowd themselves behind the cannon
10 of Fort St George.

     There were the means indeed of assembling an army
which might have defended the presidency, and even driven
the invader back to his mountains. Sir Hector Munro was
at the head of one considerable force; Baillie was advancing
15 with another. United, they might have presented a formidable front even to such an enemy as Hyder. But the
English commanders, neglecting those fundamental rules of
the military art of which the propriety is obvious even to
men who had never received a military education, deferred
20 their junction, and were separately attacked. Baillie's de-
tachment was destroyed. Munro was forced to abandon
his baggage, to fling his guns into the tanks, and to save
himself by a retreat which might be called a flight. In
three weeks from the commencement of the war, the
25 British empire in Southern India had been brought to the
verge of ruin. Only a few fortified places remained to us.
The glory of our arms had departed. It was known that
a great French expedition might soon be expected on the
coast of Coromandel. England, beset by enemies on
30 every side, was in no condition to protect such remote
dependencies.

     Then it was that the fertile genius and serene courage of
Hastings achieved their most signal triumph. A swift ship,

flying before the south-west monsoon, brought the evil
tidings in few days to Calcutta.   In twenty-four hours the
Governor-General had framed a complete plan of policy
adapted to the altered state of affairs.   The struggle with
Hyder was a struggle for life and death.   All minor objects 5
must be sacrificed to the preservation of the Carnatic.   The
disputes with the Mahrattas must be accommodated. A large
military force and a supply of money must be instantly sent
to Madras.   But even these measures would be insufficient,
unless the war, hitherto so grossly mismanaged, were placed 10
under the direction of a vigorous mind.   It was no time for
trifling. Hastings determined to resort to an extreme exercise
of power, to suspend the incapable governor of Fort St
George, to send Sir Eyre Coote to oppose Hyder, and to in-
trust that distinguished general with the whole administration 15
of the war.

     In spite of the sullen opposition of Francis, who had
now recovered from his wound, and had returned to the
Council, the Governor-General's wise and firm policy was
approved by the majority of the board. The reinforcements 20
were sent off with great expedition, and reached Madras
before the French armament arrived in the Indian seas.
Coote, broken by age and disease, was no longer the Coote
of Wandewash ; but he was still a resolute and skilful commander.   The progress of Hyder was arrested ; and in a 25
few months the great victory of Porto Novo retrieved the
honour of the English arms.

     In the mean time Francis had returned to England, and
Hastings was now left perfectly unfettered.   Wheler had
gradually been relaxing in his opposition, and, after the 30
departure of his vehement and implacable colleague, co-
operated heartily with the Governor-General, whose influence over the British in India, always great, had, by the

vigour and success of his recent measures, been considerably
increased.

But, though the difficulties arising from factions within
the Council were at an end, another class of difficulties had
5 become more pressing than ever.   The financial embarrassment was extreme.   Hastings had to find the means, not
only of carrying on the government of Bengal, but of maintaining a most costly war against both Indian and European
enemies in the Carnatic, and of making remittances to
10 England.   A few years before this time he had obtained
relief by plundering the Mogul and enslaving the Rohillas;
nor were the resources of his fruitful mind by any means
exhausted.

His first design was on Benares, a city which in wealth,
15 population, dignity, and sanctity, was among the foremost of
Asia.   It was commonly believed that half a million of
human beings was crowded into that labyrinth of lofty
alleys, rich with shrines, and minarets, and balconies, and
carved oriels, to which the sacred apes clung by hundreds.
20 The traveller could scarcely make his way through the press
of holy mendicants and not less holy bulls.   The broad and
stately flights of steps which descended from these swarming
haunts to the bathing-places along the Ganges were worn
every day by the footsteps of an innumerable multitude of
25 worshippers.   The schools and temples drew crowds of
pious Hindoos from every province where the Brahminical
faith was known.   Hundreds of devotees came thither every
month to die : for it was believed that a peculiarly happy
fate awaited the man who should pass from the sacred city
30 into the sacred river.   Nor was superstition the only motive
which allured strangers to that great metropolis.   Commerce
had as many pilgrims as religion.   All along the shores of
the venerable stream lay great fleets of vessels laden with

rich merchandise. From the looms of Benares went forth
the most delicate silks that adorned the balls of St James's
and of the *Petit Trianon:* and in the bazaars the muslins of
Bengal and the sabres of Oude were mingled with the jewels
of Golconda and the shawls of Cashmere. This rich capital, 5
and the surrounding tract, had long been under the immediate rule of a Hindoo prince who rendered homage to the
Mogul emperors. During the great anarchy of India the
lords of Benares became independent of the court of Delhi,
but were compelled to submit to the authority of the Nabob 10
of Oude. Oppressed by this formidable neighbour, they
invoked the protection of the English. The English protection was given; and at length the Nabob Vizier, by a
solemn treaty, ceded all his rights over Benares to the
Company. From that time the Rajah was the vassal of the 15
government of Bengal, acknowledged its supremacy, and
engaged to send an annual tribute to Fort William. This
tribute Cheyte Sing, the reigning prince, had paid with
strict punctuality.

Respecting the precise nature of the legal relation 20
between the Company and the Rajah of Benares, there has
been much warm and acute controversy. On the one side,
it has been maintained that Cheyte Sing was merely a great
subject on whom the superior power had a right to call for
aid in the necessities of the empire. On the other side it 25
has been contended that he was an independent prince, that
the only claim which the Company had upon him was for a
fixed tribute, and that, while the fixed tribute was regularly
paid, as it assuredly was, the English had no more right to
exact any further contribution from him than to demand 30
subsidies from Holland or Denmark. Nothing is easier than
to find precedents and analogies in favour of either view.

Our own impression is that neither view is correct. It

was too much the habit of English politicians to take it for granted that there was in India a known and definite constitution by which questions of this kind were to be decided. The truth is that, during the interval which elapsed 5 between the fall of the House of Tamerlane and the establishment of the British ascendency, there was no such constitution. The old order of things had passed away: the new order of things was not yet formed. All was transition, confusion, obscurity. Everybody kept his head 10 as he best might, and scrambled for whatever he could get. There have been similar seasons in Europe. The time of the dissolution of the Carlovingian empire is an instance. Who would think of seriously discussing the question, what extent of pecuniary aid and of obedience Hugh Capet had 15 a constitutional right to demand from the Duke of Brittany or the Duke of Normandy? The words "constitutional right" had, in that state of society, no meaning. If Hugh Capet laid hands on all the possessions of the Duke of Normandy, this might be unjust and immoral; but it would 20 not be illegal, in the sense in which the ordinances of Charles the Tenth were illegal. If, on the other hand, the Duke of Normandy made war on Hugh Capet, this might be unjust and immoral; but it would not be illegal, in the sense in which the expedition of Prince Louis Bonaparte 25 was illegal.

Very similar to this was the state of India sixty years ago. Of the existing governments not a single one could lay claim to legitimacy, or could plead any other title than recent occupation. There was scarcely a province in which 30 the real sovereignty and the nominal sovereignty were not disjoined. Titles and forms were still retained which implied that the heir of Tamerlane was an absolute ruler, and that the Nabobs of the provinces were his lieutenants. In

reality, he was a captive.   The Nabobs were in some places
independent princes.   In other places, as in Bengal and the
Carnatic, they had, like their master, become mere phan-
toms, and the Company was supreme. Among the Mahrattas
again the heir of Sevajee still kept the title of Rajah; but 5
he was a prisoner, and his prime minister, the Peshwa, had
become the hereditary chief of the state.   The Peshwa, in
his turn, was fast sinking into the same degraded situation
to which he had reduced the Rajah.   It was, we believe,
impossible to find, from the Himalayas to Mysore, a single 10
government which was at once a government *de facto* and a
government *de jure*, which possessed the physical means of
making itself feared by its neighbours and subjects, and
which had at the same time the authority derived from law
and long prescription.   15

Hastings clearly discerned, what was hidden from most
of his contemporaries, that such a state of things gave
immense advantages to a ruler of great talents and few
scruples.   In every international question that could arise,
he had his option between the *de facto* ground and the 20
de jure ground ; and the probability was that one of those
grounds would sustain any claim that it might be convenient for him to make, and enable him to resist any claim
made by others.   In every controversy, accordingly, he
resorted to the plea which suited his immediate purpose, 25
without troubling himself in the least about consistency ;
and thus he scarcely ever failed to find what, to persons
of short memories and scanty information, seemed to be a
justification for what he wanted to do.   Sometimes the
Nabob of Bengal is a shadow, sometimes a monarch. 30
Sometimes the Vizier is a mere deputy, sometimes an independent potentate.   If it is expedient for the Company to
show some legal title to the revenues of Bengal, the grant

under the seal of the Mogul is brought forward as an
instrument of the highest authority.   When the Mogul
asks for the rents which were reserved to him by that very
grant, he is told that he is a mere pageant, that the English
5 power rests on a very different foundation from a charter
given by him, that he is welcome to play at royalty as long
as he likes, but that he must expect no tribute from the real
masters of India.

   It is true that it was in the power of others, as well as
10 of Hastings, to practise this legerdemain ; but in the con-
troversies of governments, sophistry is of little use unless it
be backed by power.   There is a principle which Hastings
was fond of asserting in the strongest terms, and on which
he acted with undeviating steadiness.   It is a principle
15 which, we must own, though it may be grossly abused, can
hardly be disputed in the present state of public law.   It is
this, that where an ambiguous question arises between two
governments, there is, if they cannot agree, no appeal except
to force, and that the opinion of the stronger must prevail.
20 Almost every question was ambiguous in India.   The English
government was the strongest in India.   The consequences
are obvious.   The English government might do exactly
what it chose.

   The English government now chose to wring money out
25 of Cheyte Sing.   It had formerly been convenient to treat
him as a sovereign prince ; it was now convenient to treat
him as a subject.   Dexterity inferior to that of Hastings
could easily find, in the general chaos of laws and customs,
arguments for either course.   Hastings wanted a great
30 supply.   It was known that Cheyte Sing had a large
revenue, and it was suspected that he had accumulated
a treasure.   Nor was he a favourite at Calcutta.   He had,
when the Governor-General was in great difficulties, courted

the favour of Francis and Clavering. Hastings who, less
we believe from evil passions than from policy, seldom left
an injury unpunished, was not sorry that the fate of Cheyte
Sing should teach neighbouring princes the same lesson
which the fate of Nuncomar had already impressed on the 5
inhabitants of Bengal.

In 1778, on the first breaking out of the war with
France, Cheyte Sing was called upon to pay, in addition to
his fixed tribute, an extraordinary contribution of fifty thousand pounds. In 1779, an equal sum was exacted. In 10
1780, the demand was renewed. Cheyte Sing, in the hope
of obtaining some indulgence, secretly offered the Governor-
General a bribe of twenty thousand pounds. Hastings took
the money, and his enemies have maintained that he took it
intending to keep it. He certainly concealed the transaction, 15
for a time, both from the Council in Bengal and from the
Directors at home; nor did he ever give any satisfactory
reason for the concealment. Public spirit, or the fear of
detection, however, determined him to withstand the temptation. He paid over the bribe to the Company's treasury, 20
and insisted that the Rajah should instantly comply with the
demands of the English government. The Rajah, after the
fashion of his countrymen, shuffled, solicited, and pleaded
poverty. The grasp of Hastings was not to be so eluded.
He added to the requisition another ten thousand pounds 25
as a fine for delay, and sent troops to exact the money.

The money was paid. But this was not enough. The
late events in the south of India had increased the financial
embarrassments of the Company. Hastings was determined
to plunder Cheyte Sing, and, for that end, to fasten a 30
quarrel on him. Accordingly, the Rajah was now required
to keep a body of cavalry for the service of the British
government. He objected and evaded. This was exactly

what the Governor-General wanted.   He had now a pretext
for treating the wealthiest of his vassals as a criminal.   " I
resolved "—these are the words of Hastings himself—"to
draw from his guilt the means of relief to the Company's
5 distresses, to make him pay largely for his pardon, or to
exact a severe vengeance for past delinquency."   The plan
was simply this, to demand larger and larger contributions
till the Rajah should be driven to remonstrate, then to call
his remonstrance a crime, and to punish him by confis-
10 cating all his possessions.

Cheyte Sing was in the greatest dismay.   He offered two
hundred thousand pounds to propitiate the British government.   But Hastings replied that nothing less than half a
million would be accepted.   Nay, he began to think of
15 selling Benares to Oude, as he had formerly sold Allahabad
and Rohilcund.   The matter was one which could not be
well managed at a distance; and Hastings resolved to visit
Benares.

Cheyte Sing received his liege lord with every mark of
20 reverence, came near sixty miles, with his guards, to meet
and escort the illustrious visitor, and expressed his deep
concern at the displeasure of the English.   He even took
off his turban, and laid it in the lap of Hastings, a gesture
which in India marks the most profound submission and
25 devotion.   Hastings behaved with cold and repulsive severity.   Having arrived at Benares, he sent to the Rajah a
paper containing the demands of the government of Bengal.
The Rajah, in reply, attempted to clear himself from the
accusations brought against him.   Hastings, who wanted
30 money and not excuses, was not to be put off by the ordinary artifices of Eastern negotiation.   He instantly ordered
the Rajah to be arrested and placed under the custody of
two companies of sepoys.

In taking these strong measures, Hastings scarcely showed his usual judgment. It is probable that, having had little opportunity of personally observing any part of the population of India, except the Bengalees, he was not fully aware of the difference between their character and that of 5 the tribes which inhabit the upper provinces. He was now in a land far more favourable to the vigour of the human frame than the Delta of the Ganges; in a land fruitful of soldiers, who have been found worthy to follow English battalions to the charge and into the breach. The Rajah 10 was popular among his subjects. His administration had been mild; and the prosperity of the district which he governed presented a striking contrast to the depressed state of Bahar under our rule, and a still more striking contrast to the misery of the provinces which were cursed 15 by the tyranny of the Nabob Vizier. The national and religious prejudices with which the English were regarded throughout India were peculiarly intense in the metropolis of the Brahminical superstition. It can therefore scarcely be doubted that the Governor-General, before he outraged 20 the dignity of Cheyte Sing by an arrest, ought to have assembled a force capable of bearing down all opposition. This had not been done. The handful of sepoys who attended Hastings would probably have been sufficient to overawe Moorshedabad, or the Black Town of Calcutta. 25 But they were unequal to a conflict with the hardy rabble of Benares. The streets surrounding the palace were filled by an immense multitude, of whom a large proportion, as is usual in Upper India, wore arms. The tumult became a fight, and the fight a massacre. The English officers 30 defended themselves with desperate courage against overwhelming numbers, and fell, as became them, sword in hand. The sepoys were butchered. The gates were forced.

The captive prince, neglected by his jailers during the confusion, discovered an outlet which opened on the precipitous
bank of the Ganges, let himself down to the water by a
string made of the turbans of his attendants, found a boat,
5 and escaped to the opposite shore.

If Hastings had, by indiscreet violence, brought himself
into a difficult and perilous situation, it is only just to
acknowledge that he extricated himself with even more than
his usual ability and presence of mind. He had only fifty
10 men with him. The building in which he had taken up his
residence was on every side blockaded by the insurgents.
But his fortitude remained unshaken. The Rajah from the
other side of the river sent apologies and liberal offers.
They were not even answered. Some subtle and enterpris-
15 ing men were found who undertook to pass through the
throng of enemies, and to convey the intelligence of the
late events to the English cantonments. It is the fashion of
the natives of India to wear large earrings of gold. When
they travel, the rings are laid aside, lest the precious metal
20 should tempt some gang of robbers, and, in place of the ring,
a quill or a roll of paper is inserted in the orifice to prevent
it from closing. Hastings placed in the ears of his messengers
letters rolled up in the smallest compass. Some of these
letters were addressed to the commanders of the English
25 troops. One was written to assure his wife of his safety.
One was to the envoy whom he had sent to negotiate with
the Mahrattas. Instructions for the negotiation were needed;
and the Governor-General framed them in that situation of
extreme danger, with as much composure as if he had been
30 writing in his palace at Calcutta.

Things, however, were not yet at the worst. An English
officer of more spirit than judgment, eager to distinguish
himself, made a premature attack on the insurgents beyond

the river. His troops were entangled in narrow streets, and
assailed by a furious population. He fell, with many of his
men; and the survivors were forced to retire.

This event produced the effect which has never failed to
follow every check, however slight, sustained in India by the 5
English arms. For hundreds of miles round, the whole
country was in commotion. The entire population of the
district of Benares took arms. The fields were abandoned
by the husbandmen, who thronged to defend their prince.
The infection spread to Oude. The oppressed people of that 10
province rose up against the Nabob Vizier, refused to pay
their imposts, and put the revenue officers to flight. Even
Bahar was ripe for revolt. The hopes of Cheyte Sing began
to rise. Instead of imploring mercy in the humble style of
a vassal, he began to talk the language of a conqueror, and 15
threatened, it was said, to sweep the white usurpers out of
the land. But the English troops were now assembling fast.
The officers, and even the private men, regarded the
Governor-General with enthusiastic attachment, and flew to
his aid with an alacrity which, as he boasted, had never been 20
shown on any other occasion. Major Popham, a brave and
skilful soldier, who had highly distinguished himself in the
Mahratta war, and in whom the Governor-General reposed
the greatest confidence, took the command. The tumultuary
army of the Rajah was put to rout. His fastnesses were 25
stormed. In a few hours, above thirty thousand men left
his standard, and returned to their ordinary avocations.
The unhappy prince fled from his country for ever. His
fair domain was added to the British dominions. One of
his relations indeed was appointed rajah; but the Rajah 30
of Benares was henceforth to be, like the Nabob of Bengal,
a mere pensioner.

By this revolution, an addition of two hundred thousand

pounds a year was made to the revenues of the Company.
But the immediate relief was not as great as had been
expected. The treasure laid up by Cheyte Sing had been
popularly estimated at a million sterling. It turned out
5 to be about a fourth part of that sum ; and, such as it
was, it was seized by the army, and divided as prize-
money.

Disappointed in his expectations from Benares, Hastings
was more violent than he would otherwise have been in
10 his dealings with Oude. Sujah Dowlah had long been
dead. His son and successor, Asaph-ul-Dowlah, was one
of the weakest and most vicious even of Eastern princes.
His life was divided between torpid repose and the most
odious forms of sensuality. In his court there was bound-
15 less waste, throughout his dominions wretchedness and
disorder. He had been, under the skilful management of
the English government, gradually sinking from the rank
of an independent prince to that of a vassal of the Company. It was only by the help of a British brigade that he
20 could be secure from the aggressions of neighbours who
despised his weakness, and from the vengeance of subjects
who detested his tyranny. A brigade was furnished ; and
he engaged to defray the charge of paying and maintaining
it. From that time his independence was at an end.
25 Hastings was not a man to lose the advantage which he
had thus gained. The Nabob soon began to complain of
the burden which he had undertaken to bear. His revenues,
he said, were falling off; his servants were unpaid ; he
could no longer support the expense of the arrangement
30 which he had sanctioned. Hastings would not listen to
these representations. The Vizier, he said, had invited the
Government of Bengal to send him troops, and had promised to pay for them. The troops had been sent. How

long the troops were to remain in Oude was a matter not
settled by the treaty.   It remained, therefore, to be settled
between the contracting parties.   But the contracting parties
differed.   Who then must decide?   The stronger.

Hastings also argued that, if the English force was 5
withdrawn, Oude would certainly become a prey to anarchy,
and would probably be overrun by a Mahratta army.   That
the finances of Oude were embarrassed he admitted.   But
he contended, not without reason, that the embarrassment
was to be attributed to the incapacity and vices of Asaph-ul- 10
Dowlah himself, and that, if less were spent on the troops,
the only effect would be that more would be squandered on
worthless favourites.

Hastings had intended, after settling the affairs of Benares,
to visit Lucknow, and there to confer with Asaph-ul-Dowlah. 15
But the obsequious courtesy of the Nabob Vizier prevented
this visit.   With a small train he hastened to meet the
Governor-General.   An interview took place in the fortress
which, from the crest of the precipitous rock of Chunar,
looks down on the waters of the Ganges.   20

At first sight it might appear impossible that the negotiation should come to an amicable close.   Hastings wanted
an extraordinary supply of money.   Asaph-ul-Dowlah wanted
to obtain a remission of what he already owed.   Such a
difference seemed to admit of no compromise.   There was, 25
however, one course satisfactory to both sides, one course
by which it was possible to relieve the finances both of
Oude and of Bengal; and that course was adopted.   It was
simply this, that the Governor-General and the Nabob Vizier
should join to rob a third party; and the third party whom 30
they determined to rob was the parent of one of the
robbers.

The mother of the late Nabob, and his wife, who was

the mother of the present Nabob, were known as the
Begums or Princesses of Oude. They had possessed great
influence over Sujah Dowlah, and had, at his death, been
left in possession of a splendid dotation. The domains of
5 which they received the rents and administered the government were of wide extent. The treasure hoarded by the
late Nabob, a treasure which was popularly estimated at
near three millions sterling, was in their hands. They
continued to occupy his favourite palace at Fyzabad, the
10 Beautiful Dwelling; while Asaph-ul-Dowlah held his court in
the stately Lucknow, which he had built for himself on the
shores of the Goomti, and had adorned with noble mosques
and colleges.

Asaph-ul-Dowlah had already extorted considerable sums
15 from his mother. She had at length appealed to the English;
and the English had interfered. A solemn compact had
been made, by which she consented to give her son some
pecuniary assistance, and he in his turn promised never to
commit any further invasion of her rights. This compact
20 was formally guaranteed by the government of Bengal. But
times had changed; money was wanted; and the power
which had given the guarantee was not ashamed to instigate
the spoiler to excesses such that even he shrank from
them.

25   It was necessary to find some pretext for a confiscation
inconsistent, not merely with plighted faith, not merely with
the ordinary rules of humanity and justice, but also with
that great law of filial piety which, even in the wildest tribes
of savages, even in those more degraded communities which
30 wither under the influence of a corrupt half-civilization,
retains a certain authority over the human mind. A pretext
was the last thing that Hastings was likely to want. The
insurrection at Benares had produced disturbances in Oude.

These disturbances it was convenient to impute to the
Princesses. Evidence for the imputation there was scarcely
any; unless reports wandering from one mouth to another,
and gaining something by every transmission, may be called
evidence. The accused were furnished with no charge; 5
they were permitted to make no defence; for the Governor-
General wisely considered that, if he tried them, he might
not be able to find a ground for plundering them. It was
agreed between him and the Nabob Vizier that the noble
ladies should, by a sweeping measure of confiscation, be 10
stripped of their domains and treasures for the benefit of
the Company, and that the sums thus obtained should be
accepted by the government of Bengal in satisfaction of its
claims on the government of Oude.

While Asaph-ul-Dowlah was at Chunar, he was completely 15
subjugated by the clear and commanding intellect of the
English statesman. But when they had separated, the Vizier
began to reflect with uneasiness on the engagement into
which he had entered. His mother and grandmother protested and implored. His heart, deeply corrupted by absolute 20
power and licentious pleasures, yet not naturally unfeeling,
failed him in this crisis. Even the English resident at
Lucknow, though hitherto devoted to Hastings, shrank from
extreme measures. But the Governor-General was inex-
orable. He wrote to the resident in terms of the greatest 25
severity, and declared that, if the spoliation which had been
agreed upon were not instantly carried into effect, he would
himself go to Lucknow, and do that from which feebler
minds recoil with dismay. The resident, thus menaced,
waited on his Highness, and insisted that the treaty of 30
Chunar should be carried into full and immediate effect.
Asaph-ul-Dowlah yielded, making at the same time a solemn
protestation that he yielded to compulsion. The lands were

resumed; but the treasure was not so easily obtained. It was necessary to use violence. A body of the Company's troops marched to Fyzabad, and forced the gates of the palace. The Princesses were confined to their own apart-
5 ments. But still they refused to submit. Some more stringent mode of coercion was to be found. A mode was found of which, even at this distance of time, we cannot speak without shame and sorrow.

There were at Fyzabad two ancient men, belonging to
10 that unhappy class which a practice, of immemorial antiquity in the East, has excluded from the pleasures of love and from the hope of posterity. It has always been held in Asiatic courts that beings thus estranged from sympathy with their kind are those whom princes may most safely
15 trust. Sujah Dowlah had been of this opinion. He had given his entire confidence to the two eunuchs; and after his death they remained at the head of the household of his widow.

These two men were, by the orders of the British
20 government, seized, imprisoned, ironed, starved almost to death, in order to extort money from the Princesses. After they had been two months in confinement, their health gave way. They implored permission to take a little exercise in the garden of their prison. The officer who was in charge
25 of them stated that, if they were allowed this indulgence, there was not the smallest chance of their escaping, and that their irons really added nothing to the security of the custody in which they were kept. He did not understand the plan of his superiors. Their object in these inflictions
30 was not security but torture; and all mitigation was refused. Yet this was not the worst. It was resolved by an English government that these two infirm old men should be de- livered to the tormentors. For that purpose they were

removed to Lucknow. What horrors their dungeon there witnessed can only be guessed. But there remains on the records of Parliament, this letter, written by a British resident to a British soldier.

"Sir, the Nabob having determined to inflict corporal 5 punishment upon the prisoners under your guard, this is to desire that his officers, when they shall come, may have free access to the prisoners, and be permitted to do with them as they shall see proper."

While these barbarities were perpetrated at Lucknow, 10 the Princesses were still under duresse at Fyzabad. Food was allowed to enter their apartments only in such scanty quantities that their female attendants were in danger of perishing with hunger. Month after month this cruelty continued, till at length, after twelve hundred thousand 15 pounds had been wrung out of the Princesses, Hastings began to think that he had really got to the bottom of their revenue, and that no rigour could extort more. Then at length the wretched men who were detained at Lucknow regained their liberty. When their irons were knocked off, 20 and the doors of their prison opened, their quivering lips, the tears which ran down their cheeks, and the thanksgivings which they poured forth to the common Father of Mussulmans and Christians, melted even the stout hearts of the English warriors who stood by.   25

There is a man to whom the conduct of Hastings, through the whole of these proceedings, appears not only excusable but laudable. There is a man who tells us that he "must really be pardoned if he ventures to characterize as something preeminently ridiculous and wicked, the sensi- 30 bility which would balance against the preservation of British India a little personal suffering, which was applied only so long as the sufferers refused to deliver up a portion of that

wealth, the whole of which their own and their mistresses'
treason had forfeited." We cannot, we must own, envy the
reverend biographer, either his singular notion of what
constitutes preeminent wickedness, or his equally singular
5 perception of the preeminently ridiculous.   Is this the
generosity of an English soldier?   Is this the charity of a
Christian priest?   Could neither of Mr Gleig's professions
teach him the first rudiments of morality?   Or is morality a
thing which may be well enough in sermons, but which has
10 nothing to do with biography?

But we must not forget to do justice to Sir Elijah Impey's
conduct on this occasion.   It was not indeed easy for him
to intrude himself into a business so entirely alien from all
his official duties.   But there was something inexpressibly
15 alluring, we must suppose, in the peculiar rankness of the
infamy which was then to be got at Lucknow.   He hurried
thither as fast as relays of palanquin-bearers could carry
him.   A crowd of people came before him with affidavits
against the Begums, ready drawn in their hands.   Those
20 affidavits he did not read.   Some of them, indeed, he could
not read; for they were in the dialects of Northern India,
and no interpreter was employed*.   He administered the
oath to the deponents, with all possible expedition, and

* This passage has been slightly altered.   As it originally stood,
Sir Elijah Impey was described as ignorant of all the native languages
in which the depositions were drawn.   A writer who apparently has
had access to some private source of information has contradicted
this statement, and has asserted that Sir Elijah knew Persian and
Bengalee.   Some of the depositions were certainly in Persian.   Those
therefore Sir Elijah might have read if he had chosen to do so.   But
others were in the vernacular dialects of Upper India, with which it is
not alleged that he had any acquaintance.   Why the Bengalee is
mentioned it is not easy to guess.   Bengalee at Lucknow would have
been as useless as Portuguese in Switzerland.

asked not a single question, not even whether they had
perused the statements to which they swore. This work
performed, he got again into his palanquin, and posted back
to Calcutta, to be in time for the opening of term. The
cause was one which, by his own confession, lay altogether 5
out of his jurisdiction. Under the charter of justice, he had
no more right to inquire into crimes committed by natives
in Oude than the Lord President of the Court of Session of
Scotland to hold an assize at Exeter. He had no right to
try the Begums, nor did he pretend to try them. With 10
what object, then, did he undertake so long a journey?
Evidently in order that he might give, in an irregular
manner, that sanction which in a regular manner he could
not give, to the crimes of those who had recently hired him ;
and in order that a confused mass of testimony which he 15
did not sift, which he did not even read, might acquire an
authority not properly belonging to it, from the signature of
the highest judicial functionary in India.

The time was approaching, however, when he was to be
stripped of that robe which has never, since the Revolution, 20
been disgraced so foully as by him. The state of India had
for some time occupied much of the attention of the British
Parliament. Towards the close of the American war, two
committees of the Commons sat on Eastern affairs. In one
Edmund Burke took the lead. The other was under the 25
presidency of the able and versatile Henry Dundas, then
Lord Advocate of Scotland. Great as are the changes
which, during the last sixty years, have taken place in our
Asiatic dominions, the reports which those committees laid
on the table of the House will still be found most interest- 30
ing and instructive.

There was as yet no connection between the Company and
either of the great parties in the state. The ministers had

no motive to defend Indian abuses. On the contrary, it was for their interest to show, if possible, that the government and patronage of our Oriental empire might, with advantage, be transferred to themselves. The votes therefore, which, in consequence of the reports made by the two committees, were passed by the Commons, breathed the spirit of stern and indignant justice. The severest epithets were applied to several of the measures of Hastings, especially to the Rohilla war; and it was resolved, on the motion of Mr Dundas, that the Company ought to recall a Governor-General who had brought such calamities on the Indian people, and such dishonour on the British name. An Act was passed for limiting the jurisdiction of the Supreme Court. The bargain which Hastings had made with the Chief Justice was condemned in the strongest terms; and an address was presented to the King, praying that Impey might be ordered home to answer for his misdeeds.

Impey was recalled by a letter from the Secretary of State. But the proprietors of India Stock resolutely refused to dismiss Hastings from their service, and passed a resolution affirming, what was undeniably true, that they were intrusted by law with the right of naming and removing their Governor-General, and that they were not bound to obey the directions of a single branch of the legislature with respect to such nomination or removal.

Thus supported by his employers, Hastings remained at the head of the government of Bengal till the spring of 1785. His administration, so eventful and stormy, closed in almost perfect quiet. In the Council there was no regular opposition to his measures. Peace was restored to India. The Mahratta war had ceased. Hyder was no more. A treaty had been concluded with his son, Tippoo; and the Carnatic had been evacuated by the armies of Mysore.

Since the termination of the American war, England had no
European enemy or rival in the Eastern seas.

On a general review of the long administration of
Hastings, it is impossible to deny that, against the great
crimes by which it is blemished, we have to set off great 5
public services. England had passed through a perilous
crisis. She still, indeed, maintained her place in the foremost rank of European powers ; and the manner in which
she had defended herself against fearful odds had inspired
surrounding nations with a high opinion both of her spirit 10
and of her strength. Nevertheless, in every part of the
world, except one, she had been a loser. Not only had she
been compelled to acknowledge the independence of thirteen
colonies peopled by her children, and to conciliate the Irish
by giving up the right of legislating for them ; but, in the 15
Mediterranean, in the Gulf of Mexico, on the coast of
Africa, on the continent of America, she had been compelled
to cede the fruits of her victories in former wars. Spain
regained Minorca and Florida; France regained Senegal,
Goree, and several West Indian Islands. The only quarter 20
of the world in which Britain had lost nothing was the
quarter in which her interests had been committed to the
care of Hastings. In spite of the utmost exertions both of
European and Asiatic enemies, the power of our country in
the East had been greatly augmented. Benares was sub- 25
jected ; the Nabob Vizier reduced to vassalage. That our
influence had been thus extended, nay, that Fort William
and Fort St George had not been occupied by hostile armies,
was owing, if we may trust the general voice of the English
in India, to the skill and resolution of Hastings. 30

His internal administration, with all its blemishes, gives
him a title to be considered as one of the most remarkable
men in our history. He dissolved the double government.

He transferred the direction of affairs to English hands.
Out of a frightful anarchy, he educed at least a rude and
imperfect order. The whole organization by which justice
was dispensed, revenue collected, peace maintained through-
5 out a territory not inferior in population to the dominions of
Louis the Sixteenth or of the Emperor Joseph, was formed
and superintended by him. He boasted that every public
office, without exception, which existed when he left Bengal,
was his creation. It is quite true that this system, after all
10 the improvements suggested by the experience of sixty
years, still needs improvement, and that it was at first far
more defective than it now is. But whoever seriously con-
siders what it is to construct from the beginning the whole
of a machine so vast and complex as a government will allow
15 that what Hastings effected deserves high admiration. To
compare the most celebrated European ministers to him
seems to us as unjust as it would be to compare the best
baker in London with Robinson Crusoe, who, before he
could bake a single loaf, had to make his plough and his
20 harrow, his fences and his scarecrows, his sickle and his flail,
his mill and his oven.

The just fame of Hastings rises still higher, when we
reflect that he was not bred a statesman; that he was sent
from school to a counting-house; and that he was employed
25 during the prime of his manhood as a commercial agent, far
from all intellectual society.

Nor must we forget that all, or almost all, to whom, when
placed at the head of affairs, he could apply for assistance,
were persons who owed as little as himself, or less than him-
30 self, to education. A minister in Europe finds himself, on
the first day on which he commences his functions, surrounded by experienced public servants, the depositaries of
official traditions. Hastings had no such help. His own

reflection, his own energy, were to supply the place of all
Downing Street and Somerset House.   Having had no
facilities for learning, he was forced to teach.   He had
first to form himself, and then to form his instruments;
and this not in a single department, but in all the depart- 5
ments of the administration.

It must be added that, while engaged in this most arduous
task, he was constantly trammelled by orders from home,
and frequently borne down by a majority in council.   The
preservation of an Empire from a formidable combination of 10
foreign enemies, the construction of a government in all its
parts, were accomplished by him, while every ship brought
out bales of censure from his employers, and while the
records of every consultation were filled with acrimonious
minutes by his colleagues.   We believe that there never 15
was a public man whose temper was so severely tried; not
Marlborough, when thwarted by the Dutch Deputies; not
Wellington, when he had to deal at once with the Portuguese Regency, the Spanish Juntas, and Mr Percival.   But
the temper of Hastings was equal to almost any trial.   It 20
was not sweet; but it was calm.   Quick and vigorous as his
intellect was, the patience with which he endured the most
cruel vexations, till a remedy could be found, resembled the
patience of stupidity.   He seems to have been capable of
resentment, bitter and long-enduring; yet his resentment 25
so seldom hurried him into any blunder that it may be
doubted whether what appeared to be revenge was any
thing but policy.

The effect of this singular equanimity was that he always
had the full command of all the resources of one of the most 30
fertile minds that ever existed.   Accordingly no complica-
tion of perils and embarrassments could perplex him.   For
every difficulty he had a contrivance ready; and, whatever

may be thought of the justice and humanity of some of his contrivances, it is certain that they seldom failed to serve the purpose for which they were designed.

Together with this extraordinary talent for devising expedients, Hastings possessed, in a very high degree, another talent scarcely less necessary to a man in his situation; we mean the talent for conducting political controversy. It is as necessary to an English statesman in the East that he should be able to write, as it is to a minister in this country that he should be able to speak. It is chiefly by the oratory of a public man here that the nation judges of his powers. It is from the letters and reports of a public man in India that the dispensers of patronage form their estimate of him. In each case, the talent which receives peculiar encouragement is developed, perhaps at the expense of the other powers. In this country, we sometimes hear men speak above their abilities. It is not very unusual to find gentlemen in the Indian service who write above their abilities. The English politician is a little too much of a debater; the Indian politician a little too much of an essayist.

Of the numerous servants of the Company who have distinguished themselves as framers of minutes and despatches, Hastings stands at the head. He was indeed the person who gave to the official writing of the Indian governments the character which it still retains. He was matched against no common antagonist. But even Francis was forced to acknowledge, with sullen and resentful candour, that there was no contending against the pen of Hastings. And, in truth, the Governor-General's power of making out a case, of perplexing what it was inconvenient that people should understand, and of setting in the clearest point of view whatever would bear the light, was incomparable. His style must be praised with some reservation. It was in general forcible, pure, and polished; but it was sometimes, though not often, turgid, and, on one or two occasions, even bombastic. Perhaps the fondness of Hastings for Persian literature may have tended to corrupt his taste.

And, since we have referred to his literary tastes, it would 5 be most unjust not to praise the judicious encouragement which, as a ruler, he gave to liberal studies and curious researches. His patronage was extended, with prudent generosity, to voyages, travels, experiments, publications. He did little, it is true, towards introducing into India 10 the learning of the West. To make the young natives of Bengal familiar with Milton and Adam Smith, to substitute the geography, astronomy, and surgery of Europe for the dotages of the Brahminical superstition, or for the imperfect science of ancient Greece transfused through Arabian exposi- 15 tions, this was a scheme reserved to crown the beneficent administration of a far more virtuous ruler. Still, it is impossible to refuse high commendation to a man who, taken from a ledger to govern an empire, overwhelmed by public business, surrounded by people as busy as himself, 20 and separated by thousands of leagues from almost all literary society, gave, both by his example and by his munificence, a great impulse to learning. In Persian and Arabic literature he was deeply skilled. With the Sanscrit he was not himself acquainted; but those who first brought 25 that language to the knowledge of European students owed much to his encouragement. It was under his protection that the Asiatic Society commenced its honourable career. That distinguished body selected him to be its first president; but, with excellent taste and feeling, he declined the 30 honour in favour of Sir William Jones. But the chief advantage which the students of Oriental letters derived from his patronage remains to be mentioned. The Pundits of

Bengal had always looked with great jealousy on the attempts of foreigners to pry into those mysteries which were locked up in the sacred dialect. Their religion had been persecuted by the Mahommedans. What they knew 5 of the spirit of the Portuguese government might warrant them in apprehending persecution from Christians. That apprehension, the wisdom and moderation of Hastings removed. He was the first foreign ruler who succeeded in gaining the confidence of the hereditary priests of India, 10 and who induced them to lay open to English scholars the secrets of the old Brahminical theology and jurisprudence.

It is indeed impossible to deny that, in the great art of inspiring large masses of human beings with confidence and attachment, no ruler ever surpassed Hastings. If he had 15 made himself popular with the English by giving up the Bengalese to extortion and oppression, or if, on the other hand, he had conciliated the Bengalese and alienated the English, there would have been no cause for wonder. What is peculiar to him is that, being the chief of a small band of 20 strangers who exercised boundless power over a great indigenous population, he made himself beloved both by the subject many and by the dominant few. The affection felt for him by the civil service was singularly ardent and constant. Through all his disasters and perils, his brethren 25 stood by him with steadfast loyalty. The army, at the same time, loved him as armies have seldom loved any but the greatest chiefs who have led them to victory. Even in his disputes with distinguished military men, he could always count on the support of the military profession. While such 30 was his empire over the hearts of his countrymen, he enjoyed among the natives a popularity, such as other governors have perhaps better merited, but such as no other governor has been able to attain. He spoke their vernacular dialects

with facility and precision. He was intimately acquainted
with their feelings and usages. On one or two occasions,
for great ends, he deliberately acted in defiance of their
opinion; but on such occasions he gained more in their
respect than he lost in their love. In general, he carefully 5
avoided all that could shock their national or religious prejudices. His administration was indeed in many respects
faulty; but the Bengalee standard of good government was
not high. Under the Nabobs, the hurricane of Mahratta
cavalry had passed annually over the rich alluvial plain. 10
But even the Mahratta shrank from a conflict with the
mighty children of the sea; and the immense rice-harvests
of the Lower Ganges were safely gathered in, under the
protection of the English sword. The first English conquerors had been more rapacious and merciless even than 15
the Mahrattas; but that generation had passed away.
Defective as was the police, heavy as were the public
burdens, it is probable that the oldest man in Bengal could
not recollect a season of equal security and prosperity. For
the first time within living memory, the province was placed 20
under a government strong enough to prevent others from
robbing, and not inclined to play the robber itself. These
things inspired good will. At the same time, the constant
success of Hastings and the manner in which he extricated
himself from every difficulty made him an object of super- 25
stitious admiration; and the more than regal splendour
which he sometimes displayed dazzled a people who have
much in common with children. Even now, after the lapse
of more than fifty years, the natives of India still talk of
him as the greatest of the English; and nurses sing children 30
to sleep with a jingling ballad about the fleet horses and
richly caparisoned elephants of Sahib Warren Hostein.

The gravest offences of which Hastings was guilty did not

affect his popularity with the people of Bengal; for those offences were committed against neighbouring states. Those offences, as our readers must have perceived, we are not disposed to vindicate; yet, in order that the censure may be
5 justly apportioned to the transgression, it is fit that the motive of the criminal should be taken into consideration. The motive which prompted the worst acts of Hastings was misdirected and ill-regulated public spirit. The rules of justice, the sentiments of humanity, the plighted faith of
10 treaties, were in his view as nothing, when opposed to the immediate interest of the state. This is no justification, according to the principles either of morality, or of what we believe to be identical with morality, namely, far-sighted policy. Nevertheless the common sense of mankind, which
15 in questions of this sort seldom goes far wrong, will always recognise a distinction between crimes which originate in an inordinate zeal for the commonwealth, and crimes which originate in selfish cupidity. To the benefit of this distinction Hastings is fairly entitled. There is, we conceive, no
20 reason to suspect that the Rohilla war, the revolution of Benares, or the spoliation of the Princesses of Oude, added a rupee to his fortune. We will not affirm that, in all pecuniary dealings, he showed that punctilious integrity, that dread of the faintest appearance of evil, which is now the
25 glory of the Indian civil service. But when the school in which he had been trained and the temptations to which he was exposed are considered, we are more inclined to praise him for his general uprightness with respect to money, than rigidly to blame him for a few transactions which would
30 now be called indelicate and irregular, but which even now would hardly be designated as corrupt. A rapacious man he certainly was not. Had he been so, he would infallibly have returned to his country the richest subject in Europe. We

speak within compass, when we say that, without applying any extraordinary pressure, he might easily have obtained from the zemindars of the Company's provinces and from neighbouring princes, in the course of thirteen years, more than three millions sterling, and might have outshone the 5 splendour of Carlton House and of the *Palais Royal.* He brought home a fortune such as a Governor-General, fond of state, and careless of thrift, might easily, during so long a tenure of office, save out of his legal salary. Mrs Hastings, we are afraid, was less scrupulous. It was generally be- 10 lieved that she accepted presents with great alacrity, and that she thus formed, without the connivance of her husband, a private hoard amounting to several lacs of rupees. We are the more inclined to give credit to this story, because Mr Gleig, who cannot but have heard it, does not, so far as 15 we have observed, notice or contradict it.

The influence of Mrs Hastings over her husband was indeed such that she might easily have obtained much larger sums than she was ever accused of receiving. At length her health began to give way; and the Governor-General, much 20 against his will, was compelled to send her to England. He seems to have loved her with that love which is peculiar to men of strong minds, to men whose affection is not easily won or widely diffused. The talk of Calcutta ran for some time on the luxurious manner in which he fitted up the 25 round-house of an Indiaman for her accommodation, on the profusion of sandal-wood and carved ivory which adorned her cabin, and on the thousands of rupees which had been expended in order to procure for her the society of an agreeable female companion during the voyage. We may remark 30 here that the letters of Hastings to his wife are exceedingly characteristic. They are tender, and full of indications of esteem and confidence; but, at the same time, a little more

ceremonious than is usual in so intimate a relation.   The
solemn courtesy with which he compliments " his elegant
Marian " reminds us now and then of the dignified air with
which Sir Charles Grandison bowed over Miss Byron's hand
5 in the cedar parlour.

After some months Hastings prepared to follow his wife
to England.   When it was announced that he was about to
quit his office, the feeling of the society which he had so long
governed manifested itself by many signs.   Addresses poured
10 in from Europeans and Asiatics, from civil functionaries,
soldiers, and traders.   On the day on which he delivered up
the keys of office, a crowd of friends and admirers formed a
lane to the quay where he embarked.   Several barges escorted
him far down the river ; and some attached friends refused
15 to quit him till the low coast of Bengal was fading from the
view, and till the pilot was leaving the ship.

Of his voyage little is known, except that he amused himself with books and with his pen ; and that, among the compositions by which he beguiled the tediousness of that long
20 leisure, was a pleasing imitation of Horace's *Otium Divos
rogat.*   This little poem was inscribed to Mr Shore, afterwards Lord Teignmouth, a man of whose integrity, humanity,
and honour, it is impossible to speak too highly ; but who,
like some other excellent members of the civil service, ex-
25 tended to the conduct of his friend Hastings an indulgence
of which his own conduct never stood in need.

The voyage was, for those times, very speedy.   Hastings
was little more than four months on the sea.   In June, 1785,
he landed at Plymouth, posted to London, appeared at Court,
30 paid his respects in Leadenhall Street, and then retired with
his wife to Cheltenham.

He was greatly pleased with his reception.   The King
treated him with marked distinction.   The Queen, who had

already incurred much censure on account of the favour
which, in spite of the ordinary severity of her virtue, she
had shown to the "elegant Marian," was not less gracious
to Hastings. The Directors received him in a solemn sitting;
and their chairman read to him a vote of thanks which they 5
had passed without one dissentient voice. "I find myself,"
said Hastings, in a letter written about a quarter of a year
after his arrival in England, "I find myself every where, and
universally, treated with evidences, apparent even to my own
observation, that I possess the good opinion of my country." 10

The confident and exulting tone of his correspondence
about this time is the more remarkable, because he had
already received ample notice of the attack which was in
preparation. Within a week after he landed at Plymouth,
Burke gave notice in the House of Commons of a motion 15
seriously affecting a gentleman lately returned from India.
The session, however, was then so far advanced, that it was
impossible to enter on so extensive and important a subject.

Hastings, it is clear, was not sensible of the danger of his
position. Indeed that sagacity, that judgment, that readi- 20
ness in devising expedients, which had distinguished him
in the East, seemed now to have forsaken him; not that
his abilities were at all impaired; not that he was not
still the same man who had triumphed over Francis and
Nuncomar, who had made the Chief Justice and the Nabob 25
Vizier his tools, who had deposed Cheyte Sing, and repelled
Hyder Ali. But an oak, as Mr Grattan finely said, should
not be transplanted at fifty. A man who, having left England when a boy, returns to it after thirty or forty years
passed in India, will find, be his talents what they may, 30
that he has much both to learn and to unlearn before he
can take a place among English statesmen. The working
of a representative system, the war of parties, the arts of

debate, the influence of the press, are startling novelties to him. Surrounded on every side by new machines and new tactics, he is as much bewildered as Hannibal would have been at Waterloo, or Themistocles at Trafalgar. His very 5 acuteness deludes him. His very vigour causes him to stumble. The more correct his maxims, when applied to the state of society to which he is accustomed, the more certain they are to lead him astray. This was strikingly the case with Hastings. In India he had a bad hand; 10 but he was master of the game, and he won every stake. In England he held excellent cards, if he had known how to play them; and it was chiefly by his own errors that he was brought to the verge of ruin.

Of all his errors the most serious was perhaps the choice 15 of a champion. Clive, in similar circumstances, had made a singularly happy selection. He put himself into the hands of Wedderburn, afterwards Lord Loughborough, one of the few great advocates who have also been great in the House of Commons. To the defence of Clive, therefore, nothing 20 was wanting, neither learning nor knowledge of the world, neither forensic acuteness nor that eloquence which charms political assemblies. Hastings intrusted his interests to a very different person, a major in the Bengal army, named Scott. This gentleman had been sent over from India some 25 time before as the agent of the Governor-General. It was rumoured that his services were rewarded with Oriental munificence; and we believe that he received much more than Hastings could conveniently spare. The major obtained a seat in Parliament, and was there regarded as the 30 organ of his employer. It was evidently impossible that a gentleman so situated could speak with the authority which belongs to an independent position. Nor had the agent of Hastings the talents necessary for obtaining the ear of an assembly which, accustomed to listen to great orators, had naturally become fastidious. He was always on his legs ; he was very tedious ; and he had only one topic, the merits and wrongs of Hastings. Every body who knows the House of Commons will easily guess what followed. The Major was 5 soon considered as the greatest bore of his time. His exertions were not confined to Parliament. There was hardly a day on which the newspapers did not contain some puff upon Hastings signed *Asiaticus* or *Bengalensis*, but known to be written by the indefatigable Scott ; and 10 hardly a month in which some bulky pamphlet on the same subject, and from the same pen, did not pass to the trunk-makers and the pastry-cooks. As to this gentleman's capacity for conducting a delicate question through Parliament, our readers will want no evidence beyond that which 15 they will find in letters preserved in these volumes. We will give a single specimen of his temper and judgment. He designated the greatest man then living as " that reptile Mr Burke."

In spite, however, of this unfortunate choice, the general 20 aspect of affairs was favourable to Hastings. The King was on his side. The Company and its servants were zealous in his cause. Among public men he had many ardent friends. Such were Lord Mansfield, who had outlived the vigour of his body, but not that of his mind ; and 25 Lord Lansdowne, who, though unconnected with any party, retained the importance which belongs to great talents and knowledge. The ministers were generally believed to be favourable to the late Governor-General. They owed their power to the clamour which had been 30 raised against Mr Fox's East India Bill. The authors of that bill, when accused of invading vested rights, and of setting up powers unknown to the constitution, had defended themselves by pointing to the crimes of Hastings, and by arguing that abuses so extraordinary justified extraordinary measures. Those who, by opposing that bill, had raised themselves to the head of affairs, would 5 naturally be inclined to extenuate the evils which had been made the plea for administering so violent a remedy; and such, in fact, was their general disposition. The Lord Chancellor Thurlow, in particular, whose great place and force of intellect gave him a weight in the government 10 inferior only to that of Mr Pitt, espoused the cause of Hastings with indecorous violence. Mr Pitt, though he had censured many parts of the Indian system, had studiously abstained from saying a word against the late chief of the Indian government. To Major Scott, indeed, 15 the young minister had in private extolled Hastings as a great, a wonderful man, who had the highest claims on the government. There was only one objection to granting all that so eminent a servant of the public could ask. The resolution of censure still remained on the Journals 20 of the House of Commons. That resolution was, indeed, unjust; but, till it was rescinded, could the minister advise the King to bestow any mark of approbation on the person censured? If Major Scott is to be trusted, Mr Pitt declared that this was the only reason which 25 prevented the government from conferring a peerage on the late Governor-General. Mr Dundas was the only important member of the administration who was deeply committed to a different view of the subject. He had moved the resolutions which created the difficulty; but even from him 30 little was to be apprehended. Since he presided over the committee on Eastern affairs, great changes had taken place. He was surrounded by new allies; he had fixed his hopes on new objects; and whatever may have been his good qualities,—and he had many,—flattery itself never reckoned rigid consistency in the number.

From the ministry, therefore, Hastings had every reason to expect support; and the ministry was very powerful. The Opposition was loud and vehement against him. But 5 the Opposition, though formidable from the wealth and influence of some of its members, and from the admirable talents and eloquence of others, was outnumbered in parliament, and odious throughout the country. Nor, as far as we can judge, was the Opposition generally desirous to 10 engage in so serious an undertaking as the impeachment of an Indian Governor. Such an impeachment must last for years. It must impose on the chiefs of the party an immense load of labour. Yet it could scarcely, in any manner, affect the event of the great political game. The 15 followers of the coalition were therefore more inclined to revile Hastings than to prosecute him. They lost no opportunity of coupling his name with the names of the most hateful tyrants of whom history makes mention. The wits of Brooks's aimed their keenest sarcasms both at his 20 public and at his domestic life. Some fine diamonds which he had presented, as it was rumoured, to the royal family, and a certain richly carved ivory bed which the Queen had done him the honour to accept from him, were favourite subjects of ridicule. One lively poet proposed 25 that the great acts of the fair Marian's present husband should be immortalized by the pencil of his predecessor; and that Imhoff should be employed to embellish the House of Commons with paintings of the bleeding Rohillas, of Nuncomar swinging, of Cheyte Sing letting himself 30 down to the Ganges. Another, in an exquisitely humorous parody of Virgil's third eclogue, propounded the question what that mineral could be of which the rays had power

to make the most austere of princesses the friend of a
wanton.   A third described, with gay malevolence, the
gorgeous appearance of Mrs Hastings at St James's, the
galaxy of jewels, torn from Indian Begums, which adorned
5 her head-dress, her necklace gleaming with future votes,
and the depending questions that shone upon her ears.
Satirical attacks of this description, and perhaps a motion for
a vote of censure, would have satisfied the great body of the
Opposition.   But there were two men whose indignation was
10 not to be so appeased, Philip Francis and Edmund Burke.

   Francis had recently entered the House of Commons,
and had already established a character there for industry
and talent.   He laboured indeed under one most unfortunate defect, want of fluency.   But he occasionally
15 expressed himself with a dignity and energy worthy of the
greatest orators.   Before he had been many days in parliament, he incurred the bitter dislike of Pitt, who constantly
treated him with as much asperity as the laws of debate
would allow.   Neither lapse of years nor change of scene
20 had mitigated the enmities which Francis had brought back
from the East.   After his usual fashion, he mistook his
malevolence for virtue, nursed it, as preachers tell us that
we ought to nurse our good dispositions, and paraded it, on
all occasions, with Pharisaical ostentation.

25   The zeal of Burke was still fiercer; but it was far purer.
Men unable to understand the elevation of his mind have
tried to find out some discreditable motive for the vehemence and pertinacity which he showed on this occasion.
But they have altogether failed.   The idle story that he had
30 some private slight to revenge has long been given up, even
by the advocates of Hastings.   Mr Gleig supposes that
Burke was actuated by party spirit, that he retained a bitter
remembrance of the fall of the coalition, that he attributed

that fall to the exertions of the East India interest, and that
he considered Hastings as the head and the representative
of that interest. This explanation seems to be sufficiently
refuted by a reference to dates. The hostility of Burke to
Hastings commenced long before the coalition; and lasted 5
long after Burke had become a strenuous supporter of those
by whom the coalition had been defeated. It began when
Burke and Fox, closely allied together, were attacking the
influence of the crown, and calling for peace with the
American republic. It continued till Burke, alienated from 10
Fox, and loaded with the favours of the crown, died,
preaching a crusade against the French republic. It seems
absurd to attribute to the events of 1784 an enmity which
began in 1781, and which retained undiminished force long
after persons far more deeply implicated than Hastings in 15
the events of 1784 had been cordially forgiven. And why
should we look for any other explanation of Burke's conduct
than that which we find on the surface? The plain truth is
that Hastings had committed some great crimes, and that
the thought of those crimes made the blood of Burke boil in 20
his veins. For Burke was a man in whom compassion for
suffering, and hatred of injustice and tyranny, were as
strong as in Las Casas or Clarkson. And although in him,
as in Las Casas and in Clarkson, these noble feelings were
alloyed with the infirmity which belongs to human nature, 25
he is, like them, entitled to this great praise, that he devoted
years of intense labour to the service of a people with whom
he had neither blood nor language, neither religion nor
manners in common, and from whom no requital, no
thanks, no applause could be expected.   30

His knowledge of India was such as few even of those
Europeans who have passed many years in that country
have attained, and such as certainly was never attained by

any public man who had not quitted Europe. He had
studied the history, the laws, and the usages of the East
with an industry such as is seldom found united to so much
genius and so much sensibility.   Others have perhaps been
5 equally laborious, and have collected an equal mass of
materials.   But the manner in which Burke brought his
higher powers of intellect to work on statements of facts,
and on tables of figures, was peculiar to himself.   In every
part of those huge bales of Indian information which
10 repelled almost all other readers, his mind, at once philo-
sophical and poetical, found something to instruct or to
delight.   His reason analysed and digested those vast and
shapeless masses ; his imagination animated and coloured
them.   Out of darkness, and dulness, and confusion, he
15 formed a multitude of ingenious theories and vivid pictures.
He had, in the highest degree, that noble faculty whereby
man is able to live in the past and in the future, in the
distant and in the unreal.   India and its inhabitants were
not to him as to most Englishmen, mere names and
20 abstractions, but a real country and a real people.   The
burning sun, the strange vegetation of the palm and the
cocoa tree, the rice-field, the tank, the huge trees, older than
the Mogul empire, under which the village crowds assemble,
the thatched roof of the peasant's hut, the rich tracery of
25 the mosque where the imaum prays with his face to Mecca,
the drums, and banners, and gaudy idols, the devotees
swinging in the air, the graceful maiden, with the pitcher on
her head, descending the steps to the river-side, the black
faces, the long beards, the yellow streaks of sect, the turbans
30 and the flowing robes, the spears and the silver maces, the
elephants with their canopies of state, the gorgeous palanquin of the prince, and the close litter of the noble lady, all
those things were to him as the objects amidst which his

own life had been passed, as the objects which lay on the
road between Beaconsfield and St James's Street.   All
India was present to the eye of his mind, from the halls
where suitors laid gold and perfumes at the feet of sovereigns
to the wild moor where the gipsy camp was pitched, from 5
the bazars, humming like bee-hives with the crowd of
buyers and sellers, to the jungle where the lonely courier
shakes his bunch of iron rings to scare away the hyænas.
He had just as lively an idea of the insurrection at Benares
as of Lord George Gordon's riots, and of the execution of 10
Nuncomar as of the execution of Dr Dodd.   Oppression in
Bengal was to him the same thing as oppression in the
streets of London.

He saw that Hastings had been guilty of some most
unjustifiable acts.   All that followed was natural and neces- 15
sary in a mind like Burke's.   His imagination and his
passions, once excited, hurried him beyond the bounds of
justice and good sense.   His reason, powerful as it was,
became the slave of feelings which it should have controlled.
His indignation, virtuous in its origin, acquired too much of 20
the character of personal aversion.   He could see no miti-
gating circumstance, no redeeming merit.   His temper,
which, though generous and affectionate, had always been
irritable, had now been made almost savage by bodily
infirmities and mental vexations.   Conscious of great powers 25
and great virtues, he found himself, in age and poverty, a
mark for the hatred of a perfidious court and a deluded
people.   In Parliament his eloquence was out of date.   A
young generation, which knew him not, had filled the
House.   Whenever he rose to speak, his voice was drowned 30
by the unseemly interruptions of lads who were in their
cradles when his orations on the Stamp Act called forth the
applause of the great Earl of Chatham.   These things had

produced on his proud and sensitive spirit an effect at which
we cannot wonder.   He could no longer discuss any
question with calmness, or make allowance for honest
differences of opinion.   Those who think that he was more
5 violent and acrimonious in debates about India than on
other occasions are ill informed respecting the last years
of his life.   In the discussions on the Commercial Treaty
with the Court of Versailles. on the Regency, on the French
Revolution, he showed even more virulence than in con-
10 ducting the impeachment.   Indeed it may be remarked that
the very persons who called. him a mischievous maniac, for
condemning in burning words the Rohilla war and the
spoliation of the Begums, exalted him into a prophet as
soon as he began to declaim, with greater vehemence, and
15 not with greater reason, against the taking of the Bastile and
the insults offered to Marie Antoinette.   To us he appears
to have been neither a maniac in the former case, nor a
prophet in the latter, but in both cases a great and good
man, led into extravagance by a tempestuous sensibility
20 which domineered over all his faculties.

It may be doubted whether the personal antipathy of
Francis, or the nobler indignation of Burke, would have
led their party to adopt extreme measures against Hastings,
if his own conduct had been judicious.   He should have
25 felt that, great as his public services had been, he was not
faultless ; and should have been content to make his escape,
without aspiring to the honours of a triumph.   He and his
agent took a different view.   They were impatient for the
rewards which, as they conceived, were deferred only till
30 Burke's attack should be over.   They accordingly resolved
to force on a decisive action, with an enemy for whom, if
they had been wise, they would have made a bridge of
gold.   On the first day of the session of 1786, Major Scott

reminded Burke of the notice given in the preceding year, and asked whether it was seriously intended to bring any charge against the late Governor-General. This challenge left no course open to the Opposition, except to come forward as accusers, or to acknowledge themselves calum- 5 niators. The administration of Hastings had not been so blameless, nor was the great party of Fox and North so feeble, that it could be prudent to venture on so bold a defiance. The leaders of the Opposition instantly returned the only answer which they could with honour return ; and 10 the whole party was irrevocably pledged to a prosecution.

Burke began his operations by applying for papers. Some of the documents for which he asked were refused by the ministers, who, in the debate, held language such as strongly confirmed the prevailing opinion, that they 15 intended to support Hastings. In April the charges were laid on the table. They had been drawn by Burke with great ability, though in a form too much resembling that of a pamphlet. Hastings was furnished with a copy of the accusation ; and it was intimated to him that he might, 20 if he thought fit, be heard in his own defence at the bar of the Commons.

Here again Hastings was pursued by the same fatality which had attended him ever since the day when he set foot on English ground. It seemed to be decreed that this 25 man, so politic and so successful in the East, should commit nothing but blunders in Europe. Any judicious adviser would have told him that the best thing which he could do would be to make an eloquent, forcible, and affecting oration at the bar of the House; but that, if he could 30 not trust himself to speak, and found it necessary to read, he ought to be as concise as possible. Audiences accustomed to extemporaneous debating of the highest excellence

are always impatient of long written compositions. Hastings, however, sat down as he would have done at the Government-house in Bengal, and prepared a paper of immense length. That paper, if recorded on the consulta-
5 tions of an Indian administration, would have been justly praised as a very able minute. But it was now out of place It fell flat, as the best written defence must have fallen flat, on an assembly accustomed to the animated and strenuous conflicts of Pitt and Fox. The members, as soon
10 as their curiosity about the face and demeanour of so eminent a stranger was satisfied, walked away to dinner, and left Hastings to tell his story till midnight to the clerks and the Sergeant-at-arms.

All preliminary steps having been duly taken, Burke,
15 in the beginning of June, brought forward the charge relating to the Rohilla war. He acted discreetly in placing this accusation in the van ; for Dundas had formerly moved, and the House had adopted, a resolution condemning, in the most severe terms, the policy followed by Hastings with
20 regard to Rohilcund. Dundas had little, or rather nothing, to say in defence of his own consistency ; but he put a bold face on the matter, and opposed the motion. Among other things, he declared that, though he still thought the Rohilla war unjustifiable, he considered the services which Hastings
25 had subsequently rendered to the state as sufficient to atone even for so great an offence. Pitt did not speak, but voted with Dundas ; and Hastings was absolved by a hundred and nineteen votes against sixty-seven.

Hastings was now confident of victory. It seemed, in-
30 deed, that he had reason to be so. The Rohilla war was, of all his measures, that which his accusers might with greatest advantage assail. It had been condemned by the Court of Directors. It had been condemned by the House of Com-

mons. It had been condemned by Mr Dundas, who had since become the chief minister of the Crown for Indian affairs. Yet Burke, having chosen this strong ground, had been completely defeated on it. That, having failed here, he should succeed on any point, was generally thought impossible. It was rumoured at the clubs and coffee-houses that one or perhaps two more charges would be brought forward, that if, on those charges, the sense of the House of Commons should be against impeachment, the Opposition would let the matter drop, that Hastings would be imme- diately raised to the peerage, decorated with the star of the Bath, sworn of the privy council, and invited to lend the assistance of his talents and experience to the India board. Lord Thurlow, indeed, some months before, had spoken with contempt of the scruples which prevented Pitt from calling Hastings to the House of Lords; and had even said, that if the Chancellor of the Exchequer was afraid of the Commons, there was nothing to prevent the Keeper of the Great Seal from taking the royal pleasure about a patent of peerage. The very title was chosen. Hastings was to be Lord Dayles- ford. For, through all changes of scene and changes of fortune, remained unchanged his attachment to the spot which had witnessed the greatness and the fall of his family, and which had borne so great a part in the first dreams of his young ambition.

But in a very few days these fair prospects were overcast. On the thirteenth of June, Mr Fox brought forward, with great ability and eloquence, the charge respecting the treat- ment of Cheyte Sing. Francis followed on the same side. The friends of Hastings were in high spirits when Pitt rose. With his usual abundance and felicity of language, the Minister gave his opinion on the case. He maintained that the Governor-General was justified in calling on the Rajah

of Benares for pecuniary assistance, and in imposing a fine
when that assistance was contumaciously withheld.   He
also thought that the conduct of the Governor-General
during the insurrection had been distinguished by ability
5 and presence of mind.   He censured, with great bitterness,
the conduct of Francis, both in India and in Parliament,
as most dishonest and malignant.   The necessary inference
from Pitt's arguments seemed to be that Hastings ought
to be honourably acquitted; and both the friends and the
10 opponents of the Minister expected from him a declaration
to that effect.   To the astonishment of all parties, he
concluded by saying that, though he thought it right in
Hastings to fine Cheyte Sing for contumacy, yet the
amount of the fine was too great for the occasion.   On
15 this ground, and on this ground alone, did Mr Pitt,
applauding every other part of the conduct of Hastings
with regard to Benares, declare that he should vote in
favour of Mr Fox's motion.

The House was thunderstruck; and it well might be so.
20 For the wrong done to Cheyte Sing, even had it been as
flagitious as Fox and Francis contended, was a trifle when
compared with the horrors which had been inflicted on
Rohilcund.   But if Mr Pitt's view of the case of Cheyte
Sing were correct, there was no ground for an impeachment,
25 or even for a vote of censure.   If the offence of Hastings
was really no more than this, that, having a right to impose
a mulct, the amount of which mulct was not defined, but
was left to be settled by his discretion, he had, not for his
own advantage, but for that of the state, demanded too
30 much, was this an offence which required a criminal proceeding of the highest solemnity, a criminal proceeding, to
which, during sixty years, no public functionary had been
subjected?   We can see, we think, in what way a man of

sense and integrity might have been induced to take any
course respecting Hastings, except the course which Mr Pitt
took. Such a man might have thought a great example
necessary, for the preventing of injustice, and for the vin-
dicating of the national honour, and might, on that ground, 5
have voted for impeachment both on the Rohilla charge,
and on the Benares charge. Such a man might have thought
that the offences of Hastings had been atoned for by great
services, and might, on that ground, have voted against the
impeachment, on both charges. With great diffidence, we 10
give it as our opinion that the most correct course would,
on the whole, have been to impeach on the Rohilla charge,
and to acquit on the Benares charge. Had the Benares
charge appeared to us in the same light in which it appeared
to Mr Pitt, we should, without hesitation, have voted for 15
acquittal on that charge. The one course which it is in-
conceivable that any man of a tenth part of Mr Pitt's
abilities can have honestly taken was the course which he
took. He acquitted Hastings on the Rohilla charge. He
softened down the Benares charge till it became no charge 20
at all; and then he pronounced that it contained matter for
impeachment.

Nor must it be forgotten that the principal reason assigned
by the ministry for not impeaching Hastings on account of
the Rohilla war was this, that the delinquencies of the early 25
part of his administration had been atoned for by the excellence of the later part. Was it not most extraordinary
that men who had held this language could afterwards vote
that the later part of his administration furnished matter
for no less than twenty articles of impeachment? They first 30
represented the conduct of Hastings in 1780 and 1781 as so
highly meritorious that, like works of supererogation in the
Catholic theology, it ought to be efficacious for the cancelling

of former offences; and they then prosecuted him for his conduct in 1780 and 1781.

The general astonishment was the greater, because, only twenty-four hours before, the members on whom the minis-
5 ter could depend had received the usual notes from the Treasury, begging them to be in their places and to vote against Mr Fox's motion. It was asserted by Mr Hastings that, early on the morning of the very day on which the debate took place, Dundas called on Pitt, woke him, and was
10 closeted with him many hours. The result of this conference was a determination to give up the late Governor-General to the vengeance of the Opposition. It was impossible even for the most powerful minister to carry all his followers with him in so strange a course. Several persons high in office,
15 the Attorney-General, Mr Glenville, and Lord Mulgrave, divided against Mr Pitt. But the devoted adherents who stood by the head of the government without asking questions, were sufficiently numerous to turn the scale. A hundred and nineteen members voted for Mr Fox's motion;
20 seventy-nine against it. Dundas silently followed Pitt.

That good and great man, the late William Wilberforce, often related the events of this remarkable night. He described the amazement of the House, and the bitter reflections which were muttered against the Prime Minister
25 by some of the habitual supporters of government. Pitt himself appeared to feel that his conduct required some explanation. He left the treasury bench, sat for some time next to Mr Wilberforce, and very earnestly declared that he had found it impossible, as a man of conscience, to stand any
30 longer by Hastings. The business, he said, was too bad. Mr Wilberforce, we are bound to add, fully believed that his friend was sincere, and that the suspicions to which this mysterious affair gave rise were altogether unfounded.

Those suspicions, indeed, were such as it is painful to mention. The friends of Hastings, most of whom, it is to be observed, generally supported the administration, affirmed that the motive of Pitt and Dundas was jealousy. Hastings was personally a favourite with the king. He was 5 the idol of the East India Company and of its servants. If he were absolved by the Commons, seated among the Lords, admitted to the Board of Control, closely allied with the strong-minded and imperious Thurlow, was it not almost certain that he would soon draw to himself the entire 10 management of Eastern affairs? Was it not possible that he might become a formidable rival in the cabinet? It had probably got abroad that very singular communications had taken place between Thurlow and Major Scott, and that, if the First Lord of the Treasury was afraid to recommend 15 Hastings for a peerage, the Chancellor was ready to take the responsibility of that step on himself. Of all ministers, Pitt was the least likely to submit with patience to such an encroachment on his functions. If the Commons impeached Hastings, all danger was at an end. The pro- 20 ceeding, however it might terminate, would probably last some years. In the mean time, the accused person would be excluded from honours and public employments, and could scarcely venture even to pay his duty at court. Such were the motives attributed by a great part of the public 25 to the young minister, whose ruling passion was generally believed to be avarice of power.

The prorogation soon interrupted the discussions respecting Hastings. In the following year, those discussions were resumed. The charge touching the spoliation of the 30 Begums was brought forward by Sheridan, in a speech which was so imperfectly reported that it may be said to be wholly lost, but which was, without doubt, the most elaborately brilliant of all the productions of his ingenious mind. The impression which it produced was such as has never been equalled. He sat down, not merely amidst cheering, but amidst the loud clapping of hands, in which 5 the Lords below the Bar and the strangers in the gallery joined. The excitement of the House was such that no other speaker could obtain a hearing; and the debate was adjourned. The ferment spread fast through the town. Within four and twenty hours, Sheridan was offered a 10 thousand pounds for the copyright of the speech, if he would himself correct it for the press. The impression made by this remarkable display of eloquence on severe and experienced critics, whose discernment may be supposed to have been quickened by emulation, was deep and 15 permanent. Mr Windham, twenty years later, said that the speech deserved all its fame, and was, in spite of some faults of taste, such as were seldom wanting either in the literary or in the parliamentary performances of Sheridan, the finest that had been delivered within the memory of 20 man. Mr Fox, about the same time, being asked by the late Lord Holland what was the best speech ever made in the House of Commons, assigned the first place, without hesitation, to the great oration of Sheridan on the Oude charge.

25   When the debate was resumed, the tide ran so strongly against the accused that his friends were coughed and scraped down. Pitt declared himself for Sheridan's motion; and the question was carried by a hundred and seventy-five votes against sixty-eight.

30   The Opposition, flushed with victory and strongly supported by the public sympathy, proceeded to bring forward a succession of charges relating chiefly to pecuniary transactions. The friends of Hastings were discouraged, and,

having now no hope of being able to avert an impeachment, were not very strenuous in their exertions. At length the House, having agreed to twenty articles of charge, directed Burke to go before the Lords, and to impeach the late Governor-General of High Crimes and Misdemeanours. 5 Hastings was at the same time arrested by the Sergeant-at-arms, and carried to the bar of the Peers.

The session was now within ten days of its close. It was, therefore, impossible that any progress could be made in the trial till the next year. Hastings was admitted to 10 bail; and further proceedings were postponed till the Houses should re-assemble.

When Parliament met in the following winter, the Commons proceeded to elect a committee for managing the impeachment. Burke stood at the head; and with 15 him were associated most of the leading members of the Opposition. But when the name of Francis was read a fierce contention arose. It was said that Francis and Hastings were notoriously on bad terms, that they had been at feud during many years, that on one occasion their 20 mutual aversion had impelled them to seek each other's lives, and that it would be improper and indelicate to select a private enemy to be a public accuser. It was urged on the other side with great force, particularly by Mr Windham, that impartiality, though the first duty of 25 a judge, had never been reckoned among the qualities of an advocate; that in the ordinary administration of criminal justice among the English, the aggrieved party, the very last person who ought to be admitted into the jury-box, is the prosecutor; that what was wanted in a manager was, not 30 that he should be free from bias, but that he should be able, well informed, energetic, and active. The ability and information of Francis were admitted; and the very

animosity with which he was reproached, whether a virtue
or a vice, was at least a pledge for his energy and activity.
It seems difficult to refute these arguments. But the inveterate hatred borne by Francis to Hastings had excited
5 general disgust. The House decided that Francis should
not be a manager. Pitt voted with the majority, Dundas
with the minority.

In the mean time, the preparations for the trial had proceeded rapidly; and on the thirteenth of February, 1788,
10 the sittings of the Court commenced. There have been
spectacles more dazzling to the eye, more gorgeous with
jewellery and cloth of gold, more attractive to grown-up
children, than that which was then exhibited at Westminster; but, perhaps, there never was a spectacle so well
15 calculated to strike a highly cultivated, a reflecting, an
imaginative mind. All the various kinds of interest which
belong to the near and to the distant, to the present and
to the past, were collected on one spot, and in one hour.
All the talents and all the accomplishments which are
20 developed by liberty and civilization were now displayed,
with every advantage that could be derived both from
cooperation and from contrast. Every step in the proceedings carried the mind either backward, through many
troubled centuries, to the days when the foundations of
25 our constitution were laid; or far away, over boundless
seas and deserts, to dusky nations living under strange
stars, worshipping strange gods, and writing strange characters from right to left. The High Court of Parliament
was to sit, according to forms handed down from the
30 days of the Plantagenets, on an Englishman accused of
exercising tyranny over the lord of the holy city of
Benares, and over the ladies of the princely house of
Oude.

The place was worthy of such a trial. It was the great
hall of William Rufus, the hall which had resounded with
acclamations at the inauguration of thirty kings, the hall
which had witnessed the just sentence of Bacon and the
just absolution of Somers, the hall where the eloquence 5
of Strafford had for a moment awed and melted a
victorious party inflamed with just resentment, the hall
where Charles had confronted the High Court of Justice
with the placid courage which has half redeemed his
fame. Neither military nor civil pomp was wanting. The 10
avenues were lined with grenadiers. The streets were kept
clear by cavalry. The peers, robed in gold and ermine,
were marshalled by the heralds under Garter King-at-
arms. The judges in their vestments of state attended
to give advice on points of law. Near a hundred and 15
seventy lords, three-fourths of the Upper House as the
Upper House then was, walked in solemn order from their
usual place of assembling to the tribunal. The junior
baron present led the way, George Eliott, Lord Heath-
field, recently ennobled for his memorable defence of 20
Gibraltar against the fleets and armies of France and
Spain. The long procession was closed by the Duke of
Norfolk, Earl Marshal of the realm, by the great digni-
taries, and by the brothers and sons of the King. Last
of all came the Prince of Wales, conspicuous by his fine 25
person and noble bearing. The grey old walls were hung
with scarlet. The long galleries were crowded by an
audience such as has rarely excited the fears or the emulation of an orator. There were gathered together, from all
parts of a great, free, enlightened, and prosperous empire, 30
grace and female loveliness, wit and learning, the representatives of every science and of every art. There were
seated round the Queen the fair-haired young daughters

of the house of Brunswick. There the Ambassadors of
great Kings and Commonwealths gazed with admiration
on a spectacle which no other country in the world could
present. There Siddons, in the prime of her majestic
5 beauty, looked with emotion on a scene surpassing all the
imitations of the stage. There the historian of the Roman
Empire thought of the days when Cicero pleaded the cause
of Sicily against Verres, and when, before a senate which
still retained some show of freedom, Tacitus thundered
10 against the oppressor of Africa. There were seen, side
by side, the greatest painter and the greatest scholar of
the age. The spectacle had allured Reynolds from that
easel which has preserved to us the thoughtful foreheads
of so many writers and statesmen, and the sweet smiles
15 of so many noble matrons. It had induced Parr to
suspend his labours in that dark and profound mine from
which he had extracted a vast treasure of erudition, a
treasure too often buried in the earth, too often paraded
with injudicious and inelegant ostentation, but still precious,
20 massive, and splendid. There appeared the voluptuous
charms of her to whom the heir of the throne had in
secret plighted his faith. There too was she, the beautiful
mother of a beautiful race, the Saint Cecilia whose delicate
features, lighted up by love and music, art has rescued
25 from the common decay. There were the members of that
brilliant society which quoted, criticised, and exchanged
repartees, under the rich peacock-hangings of Mrs Mon-
tague. And there the ladies whose lips, more persuasive
than those of Fox himself, had carried the Westminster
30 election against palace and treasury, shone round Georgiana
Duchess of Devonshire.

    The Sergeants made proclamation. Hastings advanced
to the bar and bent his knee. The culprit was indeed not

unworthy of that great presence. He had ruled an extensive and populous country, and made laws and treaties, had sent forth armies, had set up and pulled down princes. And in his high place he had so borne himself, that all had feared him, that most had loved him, and that hatred 5 itself could deny him no title to glory, except virtue. He looked like a great man, and not like a bad man. A person small and emaciated, yet deriving dignity from a carriage which, while it indicated deference to the court, indicated also habitual self-possession and self-respect, a 10 high and intellectual forehead, a brow pensive, but not gloomy, a mouth of inflexible decision, a face pale and worn, but serene, on which was written, as legibly as under the picture in the council-chamber at Calcutta, *Mens æqua in arduis;* such was the aspect with which the great pro- 15 consul presented himself to his judges.

His counsel accompanied him, men all of whom were afterwards raised by their talents and learning to the highest posts in their profession, the bold and strong-minded Law, afterwards Chief Justice of the King's Bench; the more 20 humane and eloquent Dallas, afterwards Chief Justice of the Common Pleas; and Plomer who, near twenty years later, successfully conducted in the same high court the defence of Lord Melville, and subsequently became Vice-chancellor and Master of the Rolls. 25

But neither the culprit nor his advocates attracted so much notice as the accusers. In the midst of the blaze of red drapery, a space had been fitted up with green benches, and tables for the Commons. The managers, with Burke at their head, appeared in full dress. The collectors of 30 gossip did not fail to remark that even Fox, generally so regardless of his appearance, had paid to the illustrious tribunal the compliment of wearing a bag and sword.

Pitt had refused to be one of the conductors of the impeachment; and his commanding, copious, and sonorous eloquence was wanting to that great muster of various talents. Age and blindness had unfitted Lord North for
5 the duties of a public prosecutor; and his friends were left without the help of his excellent sense, his tact, and his urbanity. But, in spite of the absence of these two distinguished members of the Lower House, the box in which the managers stood contained an array of speakers
10 such as perhaps had not appeared together since the great age of Athenian eloquence. There were Fox and Sheridan, the English Demosthenes and the English Hyperides. There was Burke, ignorant, indeed, or negligent of the art of adapting his reasonings and his style to the capacity
15 and taste of his hearers, but in amplitude of comprehension and richness of imagination superior to every orator, ancient or modern. There, with eyes reverentially fixed on Burke, appeared the finest gentleman of the age, his form developed by every manly exercise, his face beaming
20 with intelligence and spirit, the ingenious, the chivalrous, the high-souled Windham. Nor, though surrounded by such men, did the youngest manager pass unnoticed. At an age when most of those who distinguished themselves in life are still contending for prizes and fellowships at
25 college, he had won for himself a conspicuous place in parliament. No advantage of fortune or connection was wanting that could set off to the height his splendid talents and his unblemished honour. At twenty-three he had been thought worthy to be ranked with the veteran
30 statesmen who appeared as the delegates of the British Commons, at the bar of the British nobility. All who stood at that bar, save him alone, are gone, culprit, advocates, accusers. To the generation which is now in the

vigour of life, he is the sole representative of a great age
which has passed away. But those who, within the last
ten years, have listened with delight, till the morning sun
shone on the tapestries of the House of Lords, to the lofty
and animated eloquence of Charles Earl Grey, are able to 5
form some estimate of the powers of a race of men among
whom he was not the foremost.

The charges and the answers of Hastings were first
read. The ceremony occupied two whole days, and was
rendered less tedious than it would otherwise have been 10
by the silver voice and just emphasis of Cowper, the clerk
of the court, a near relation of the amiable poet. On the
third day Burke rose. Four sittings were occupied by his
opening speech, which was intended to be a general introduction to all the charges. With an exuberance of thought 15
and a splendour of diction which more than satisfied the
highly-raised expectation of the audience, he described the
character and institutions of the natives of India, re-
counted the circumstances in which the Asiatic empire of
Britain had originated, and set forth the constitution of 20
the Company and of the English Presidencies. Having
thus attempted to communicate to his hearers an idea of
Eastern society, as vivid as that which existed in his own
mind, he proceeded to arraign the administration of Hastings as systematically conducted in defiance of morality 25
and public law. The energy and pathos of the great
orator extorted expressions of unwonted admiration from
the stern and hostile Chancellor, and, for a moment, seemed
to pierce even the resolute heart of the defendant. The
ladies in the galleries, unaccustomed to such displays of 30
eloquence, excited by the solemnity of the occasion, and
perhaps not unwilling to display their taste and sensibility, were in a state of uncontrollable emotion. Hand-

kerchiefs were pulled out; smelling-bottles were handed
round; hysterical sobs and screams were heard; and Mrs
Sheridan was carried out in a fit. At length the orator
concluded. Raising his voice till the old arches of Irish
5 oak resounded, "Therefore," said he, "hath it with all
confidence been ordered by the Commons of Great Britain,
that I impeach Warren Hastings of high crimes and misdemeanours. I impeach him in the name of the Commons'
House of Parliament, whose trust he has betrayed. I
10 impeach him in the name of the English nation, whose
ancient honour he has sullied. I impeach him in the
name of the people of India, whose rights he has trodden
under foot, and whose country he has turned into a desert.
Lastly, in the name of human nature itself, in the name
15 of both sexes, in the name of every age, in the name of
every rank, I impeach the common enemy and oppressor
of all!"

When the deep murmur of various emotions had sub-
sided, Mr Fox rose to address the Lords respecting the
20 course of proceeding to be followed. The wish of the
accusers was that the Court would bring to a close the
investigation of the first charge before the second was
opened. The wish of Hastings and of his counsel was
that the managers should open all the charges, and pro-
25 duce all the evidence for the prosecution, before the defence
began. The Lords retired to their own House to consider
the question. The Chancellor took the side of Hastings.
Lord Loughborough, who was now in opposition, supported
the demand of the managers. The division showed which
30 way the inclination of the tribunal leaned. A majority of
near three to one decided in favour of the course for which
Hastings contended.

When the Court sat again, Mr Fox, assisted by Mr Grey,

opened the charge respecting Cheyte Sing, and several days
were spent in reading papers and hearing witnesses. The
next article was that relating to the Princesses of Oude. The
conduct of this part of the case was intrusted to Sheridan.
The curiosity of the public to hear him was unbounded. 5
His sparkling and highly finished declamation lasted two
days; but the Hall was crowded to suffocation during the
whole time. It was said that fifty guineas had been paid
for a single ticket. Sheridan, when he concluded, contrived,
with a knowledge of stage-effect which his father might have 10
envied, to sink back, as if exhausted, into the arms of Burke,
who hugged him with the energy of generous admiration.

June was now far advanced. The session could not last
much longer; and the progress which had been made in the
impeachment was not very satisfactory. There were twenty 15
charges. On two only of these had even the case for the
prosecution been heard; and it was now a year since Hastings had been admitted to bail.

The interest taken by the public in the trial was great
when the Court began to sit, and rose to the height when 20
Sheridan spoke on the charge relating to the Begums. From
that time the excitement went down fast. The spectacle
had lost the attraction of novelty. The great displays of
rhetoric were over. What was behind was not of a nature
to entice men of letters from their books in the morning, or 25
to tempt ladies who had left the masquerade at two to be
out of bed before eight. There remained examinations and
cross-examinations. There remained statements of accounts.
There remained the reading of papers, filled with words unintelligible to English ears, with lacs and crores, zemindars 30
and aumils, sunnuds and perwannahs, jaghires and nuzzurs.
There remained bickerings, not always carried on with the
best taste or with the best temper, between the managers of

the impeachment and the counsel for the defence, particularly
between Mr Burke and Mr Law.   There remained the end-
less marches and counter-marches of the Peers between their
House and the Hall: for as often as a point of law was to
5 be discussed, their Lordships retired to discuss it apart ; and
the consequence was, as a peer wittily said, that the Judges
walked and the trial stood still.

It is to be added that, in the spring of 1788 when the trial
commenced, no important question, either of domestic or
10 foreign policy, excited the public mind.   The proceeding in
Westminster Hall, therefore, naturally attracted most of the
attention of Parliament and of the public.   It was the one
great event of that season.   But in the following year the
King's illness, the debates on the Regency, the expectation
15 of a change of Ministry, completely diverted public attention
from Indian affairs ; and within a fortnight after George the
Third had returned thanks in St Paul's for his recovery, the
States-General of France met at Versailles.   In the midst of
the agitation produced by these events, the impeachment
20 was for a time almost forgotten.

The trial in the Hall went on languidly.   In the session
of 1788, when the proceedings had the interest of novelty,
and when the Peers had little other business before them,
only thirty-five days were given to the impeachment.   In
25 1789, the Regency Bill occupied the Upper House till the
session was far advanced.   When the King recovered the
circuits were beginning.   The judges left town ; the Lords
waited for the return of the oracles of jurisprudence ; and
the consequence was that during the whole year only seven-
30 teen days were given to the case of Hastings.   It was clear
that the matter would be protracted to a length unprecedented in the annals of criminal law.

In truth, it is impossible to deny that impeachment,

though it is a fine ceremony, and though it may have been useful in the seventeenth century, is not a proceeding from which much good can now be expected. Whatever confidence may be placed in the decisions of the Peers on an appeal arising out of ordinary litigation, it is certain that no 5 man has the least confidence in their impartiality, when a great public functionary, charged with a great state crime, is brought to their bar. They are all politicians. There is hardly one among them whose vote on an impeachment may not be confidently predicted before a witness has been 10 examined; and, even if it were possible to rely on their justice, they would still be quite unfit to try such a cause as that of Hastings. They sit only during half the year. They have to transact much legislative and much judicial business. The law-lords, whose advice is required to guide the unlearned 15 majority, are employed daily in administering justice elsewhere. It is impossible, therefore, that during a busy session, the Upper House should give more than a few days to an impeachment. To expect that their Lordships would give up partridge-shooting, in order to bring the greatest delinquent 20 to speedy justice, or to relieve accused innocence by speedy acquittal, would be unreasonable indeed. A well-constituted tribunal, sitting regularly six days in the week, and nine hours in the day, would have brought the trial of Hastings to a close in less than three months. The Lords had not 25 finished their work in seven years.

The result ceased to be matter of doubt, from the time when the Lords resolved that they would be guided by the rules of evidence which are received in the inferior courts of the realm. Those rules, it is well known, exclude much 30 information which would be quite sufficient to determine the conduct of any reasonable man, in the most important transactions of private life. Those rules, at every assizes, save

scores of culprits whom judges, jury, and spectators, firmly
believe to be guilty.   But when those rules were rigidly
applied to offences committed many years before, at the
distance of many thousand miles, conviction was, of course,
5 out of the question.   We do not blame the accused and his
counsel for availing themselves of every legal advantage in
order to obtain an acquittal.   But it is clear that an acquittal
so obtained cannot be pleaded in bar of the judgment of
history.

10   Several attempts were made by the friends of Hastings to
put a stop to the trial.   In 1789 they proposed a vote of
censure upon Burke, for some violent language which he had
used respecting the death of Nuncomar and the connection
between Hastings and Impey.   Burke was then unpopular
15 in the last degree both with the House and with the country.
The asperity and indecency of some expressions which he
had used during the debates on the Regency had annoyed
even his warmest friends.   The vote of censure was carried;
and those who had moved it hoped that the managers would
20 resign in disgust.   Burke was deeply hurt.   But his zeal for
what he considered as the cause of justice and mercy triumphed over his personal feelings.   He received the censure
of the House with dignity and meekness, and declared that
no personal mortification or humiliation should induce him
25 to flinch from the sacred duty which he had undertaken.

In the following year the Parliament was dissolved, and
the friends of Hastings entertained a hope that the new
House of Commons might not be disposed to go on with the
impeachment.   They began by maintaining that the whole
30 proceeding was terminated by the dissolution.   Defeated on
this point, they made a direct motion that the impeachment
should be dropped ; but they were defeated by the combined
forces of the Government and the Opposition.   It was, how-

ever, resolved that, for the sake of expedition, many of the articles should be withdrawn. In truth, had not some such measure been adopted, the trial would have lasted till the defendant was in his grave.

At length, in the spring of 1795, the decision was pro- 5 nounced, near eight years after Hastings had been brought by the Sergeant-at-arms of the Commons to the bar of the Lords. On the last day of this great procedure the public curiosity, long suspended, seemed to be revived. Anxiety about the judgment there could be none; for it had been 10 fully ascertained that there was a great majority for the defendant. Nevertheless many wished to see the pageant, and the Hall was as much crowded as on the first day. But those who, having been present on the first day, now bore a part in the proceedings of the last, were few; and most of 15 those few were altered men.

As Hastings himself said, the arraignment had taken place before one generation, and the judgment was pronounced by another. The spectator could not look at the woolsack, or at the red benches of the Peers, or at the green benches of the 20 Commons, without seeing something that reminded him of the instability of all human things, of the instability of power and fame and life, of the more lamentable instability of friendship. The great seal was borne before Lord Lough-borough who, when the trial commenced, was a fierce 25 opponent of Mr Pitt's government, and who was now a member of that government, while Thurlow, who presided in the court when it first sat, estranged from all his old allies, sat scowling among the junior barons. Of about a hundred and sixty nobles who walked in the procession on 30 the first day, sixty had been laid in their family vaults. Still more affecting must have been the sight of the managers' box. What had become of that fair fellowship, so closely

bound together by public and private ties, so resplendent
with every talent and accomplishment? It had been scattered by calamities more bitter than the bitterness of death.
The great chiefs were still living, and still in the full vigour
5 of their genius. But their friendship was at an end. It had
been violently and publicly dissolved, with tears and stormy
reproaches. If those men, once so dear to each other, were
now compelled to meet for the purpose of managing the
impeachment, they met as strangers whom public business
10 had brought together, and behaved to each other with cold
and distant civility. Burke had in his vortex whirled away
Windham. Fox had been followed by Sheridan and Grey.

Only twenty-nine Peers voted. Of these only six found
Hastings guilty on the charges relating to Cheyte Sing and
15 to the Begums. On other charges, the majority in his
favour was still greater. On some, he was unanimously
absolved. He was then called to the bar, was informed from
the woolsack that the Lords had acquitted him, and was
solemnly discharged. He bowed respectfully and retired.

20   We have said that the decision had been fully expected.
It was also generally approved. At the commencement of
the trial there had been a strong and indeed unreasonable
feeling against Hastings. At the close of the trial there was
a feeling equally strong and equally unreasonable in his
25 favour. One cause of the change was, no doubt, what is
commonly called the fickleness of the multitude, but what
seems to us to be merely the general law of human nature.
Both in individuals and in masses violent excitement is
always followed by remission, and often by reaction. We
30 are all inclined to depreciate whatever we have overpraised,
and, on the other hand, to show undue indulgence where we
have shown undue rigour. It was thus in the case of
Hastings. The length of his trial, moreover, made him an

object of compassion. It was thought, and not without
reason, that, even if he was guilty, he was still an ill-used
man, and that an impeachment of eight years was more
than a sufficient punishment. It was also felt that, though,
in the ordinary course of criminal law, a defendant is not 5
allowed to set off his good actions against his crimes, a
great political cause should be tried on different principles,
and that a man who had governed an empire during
thirteen years might have done some very reprehensible
things, and yet might be on the whole deserving of rewards 10
and honours rather than of fine and imprisonment. The
press, an instrument neglected by the prosecutors, was used
by Hastings and his friends with great effect. Every ship,
too, that arrived from Madras or Bengal, brought a cuddy
full of his admirers. Every gentleman from India spoke of 15
the late Governor-General as having deserved better, and
having been treated worse, than any man living. The
effect of this testimony unanimously given by all persons
who knew the East, was naturally very great. Retired
members of the Indian services, civil and military, were 20
settled in all corners of the kingdom. Each of them was,
of course, in his own little circle, regarded as an oracle on
an Indian question; and they were, with scarcely one
exception, the zealous advocates of Hastings. It is to be
added, that the numerous addresses to the late Governor- 25
General, which his friends in Bengal obtained from the
natives and transmitted to England, made a considerable
impression. To these addresses we attach little or no
importance. That Hastings was beloved by the people
whom he governed is true; but the eulogies of pundits, 30
zemindars, Mahommedan doctors, do not prove it to be
true. For an English collector or judge would have found
it easy to induce any native who could write to sign a

panegyric on the most odious ruler that ever was in India.
It was said that at Benares, the very place at which the acts
set forth in the first article of impeachment had been committed, the natives had erected a temple to Hastings; and
5 this story excited a strong sensation in England.   Burke's
observations on the apotheosis were admirable.   He saw
no reason for astonishment, he said, in the incident which
had been represented as so striking.   He knew something
of the mythology of the Brahmins.   He knew that as they
10 worshipped some gods from love, so they worshipped others
from fear.   He knew that they erected shrines, not only to
the benignant deities of light and plenty, but also to the
fiends who preside over small-pox and murder.   Nor did he
at all dispute the claim of Mr Hastings to be admitted into
15 such a Pantheon.   This reply has always struck us as one
of the finest that ever was made in Parliament.   It is a
grave and forcible argument, decorated by the most brilliant
wit and fancy.

Hastings was, however, safe.   But in every thing except
20 character, he would have been far better off if, when first
impeached, he had at once pleaded guilty, and paid a fine
of fifty thousand pounds.   He was a ruined man.   The
legal expenses of his defence had been enormous.   The
expenses which did not appear in his attorney's bill
25 were perhaps larger still.   Great sums had been paid to
Major Scott.   Great sums had been laid out in bribing
newspapers, rewarding pamphleteers, and circulating tracts.
Burke, so early as 1790, declared in the House of Commons
that twenty thousand pounds had been employed in cor-
30 rupting the press.   It is certain that no controversial
weapon, from the gravest reasoning to the coarsest ribaldry,
was left unemployed.   Logan defended the accused governor with great ability in prose.   For the lovers of verse, the

speeches of the managers were burlesqued in Simpkin's letters. It is, we are afraid, indisputable that Hastings stooped so low as to court the aid of that malignant and filthy baboon John Williams, who called himself Anthony Pasquin. It was necessary to subsidise such allies largely. 5 The private hoards of Mrs Hastings had disappeared. It is said that the banker to whom they had been entrusted had failed. Still if Hastings had practised strict economy, he would, after all his losses, have had a moderate competence; but in the management of his private affairs he was im- 10 prudent. The dearest wish of his heart had always been to regain Daylesford. At length, in the very year in which his trial commenced, the wish was accomplished; and the domain, alienated more than seventy years before, returned to the descendant of its old lords. But the manor house 15 was a ruin; and the grounds round it had, during many years, been utterly neglected. Hastings proceeded to build, to plant, to form a sheet of water, to excavate a grotto; and, before he was dismissed from the bar of the House of Lords, he had expended more than forty thousand pounds 20 in adorning his seat.

The general feeling both of the Directors and of the proprietors of the East India Company was that he had great claims on them, that his services to them had been eminent, and that his misfortunes had been the effect of his 25 zeal for their interest. His friends in Leadenhall Street proposed to reimburse him for the costs of his trial, and to settle on him an annuity of five thousand pounds a year. But the consent of the Board of Control was necessary; and at the head of the Board of Control was Mr Dundas, who 30 had himself been a party to the impeachment, who had, on that account, been reviled with great bitterness by the adherents of Hastings, and, who, therefore, was not in a very complying mood. He refused to consent to what the Directors suggested. The Directors remonstrated. A long controversy followed. Hastings, in the mean time, was reduced to such distress, that he could hardly pay his weekly bills. At length a compromise was made. An annuity of four thousand a year was settled on Hastings; and in order to enable him to meet pressing demands, he was to receive ten years' annuity in advance. The Company was also permitted to lend him fifty thousand pounds, to be repaid by instalments without interest. This relief, though given in the most absurd manner, was sufficient to enable the retired governor to live in comfort, and even in luxury, if he had been a skilful manager. But he was careless and profuse, and was more than once under the necessity of applying to the Company for assistance, which was liberally given.

He had security and affluence, but not the power and dignity which, when he landed from India, he had reason to expect. He had then looked forward to a coronet, a red riband, a seat at the Council Board, an office at Whitehall. He was then only fifty-two, and might hope for many years of bodily and mental vigour. The case was widely different when he left the bar of the Lords. He was now too old a man to turn his mind to a new class of studies and duties. He had no chance of receiving any mark of royal favour while Mr Pitt remained in power; and, when Mr Pitt retired, Hastings was approaching his seventieth year.

Once, and only once, after his acquittal, he interfered in politics; and that interference was not much to his honour. In 1804 he exerted himself strenuously to prevent Mr Addington, against whom Fox and Pitt had combined, from resigning the Treasury. It is difficult to believe that a man so able and energetic as Hastings can have thought that,

when Bonaparte was at Boulogne with a great army, the
defence of our island could safely be entrusted to a ministry
which did not contain a single person whom flattery could
describe as a great statesman. It is also certain that, on
the important question which had raised Mr Addington to 5
power, and on which he differed from both Fox and Pitt,
Hastings, as might have been expected, agreed with Fox
and Pitt, and was decidedly opposed to Addington. Religious intolerance has never been the vice of the Indian
service, and certainly was not the vice of Hastings. But 10
Mr Addington had treated him with marked favour. Fox
had been a principal manager of the impeachment. To
Pitt it was owing that there had been an impeachment; and
Hastings, we fear, was on this occasion guided by personal
considerations, rather than by a regard to the public interest. 15

The last twenty-four years of his life were chiefly passed
at Daylesford. He amused himself with embellishing his
grounds, riding fine Arab horses, fattening prize-cattle, and
trying to rear Indian animals and vegetables in England.
He sent for seeds of a very fine custard-apple, from the 20
garden of what had once been his own villa, among the
green hedgerows of Allipore. He tried also to naturalise
in Worcestershire the delicious leechee, almost the only
fruit of Bengal which deserves to be regretted even amidst
the plenty of Covent Garden. The Mogul emperors, in the 25
time of their greatness, had in vain attempted to introduce
into Hindostan the goat of the table-land of Thibet, whose
down supplies the looms of Cashmere with the materials of
the finest shawls. Hastings tried, with no better fortune, to
rear a breed at Daylesford; nor does he seem to have 30
succeeded better with the cattle of Bootan, whose tails are
in high esteem as the best fans for brushing away the
mosquitoes.

Literature divided his attention with his conservatories and his menagerie. He had always loved books, and they were now necessary to him. Though not a poet, in any high sense of the word, he wrote neat and polished lines 5 with great facility, and was fond of exercising this talent. Indeed, if we must speak out, he seems to have been more of a Trissotin than was to be expected from the powers of his mind, and from the great part which he had played in life. We are assured in these Memoirs that the first 10 thing which he did in the morning was to compose a copy of verses. When the family and guests assembled, the poem made its appearance as regularly as the eggs and rolls; and Mr Gleig requires us to believe that, if from any accident Hastings came to the breakfast-table without one 15 of his charming performances in his hand, the omission was felt by all as a grievous disappointment. Tastes differ widely. For ourselves we must say that, however good the breakfasts at Daylesford may have been,—and we are assured that the tea was of the most aromatic flavour, and 20 that neither tongue nor venison-pasty was wanting,—we should have thought the reckoning high if we had been forced to earn our repast by listening every day to a new madrigal or sonnet composed by our host. We are glad, however, that Mr Gleig has preserved this little feature 25 of character, though we think it by no means a beauty. It is good to be often reminded of the inconsistency of human nature, and to learn to look without wonder or disgust on the weaknesses which are found in the strongest minds. Dionysius in old times, Frederic in the last century, with 30 capacity and vigour equal to the conduct of the greatest affairs, united all the little vanities and affectations of provincial blue-stockings. These great examples may console the admirers of Hastings for the affliction of

seeing him reduced to the level of the Hayleys and
Sewards.

When Hastings had passed many years in retirement,
and had long outlived the common age of men, he again
became for a short time an object of general attention.   In 5
1813 the charter of the East India Company was renewed;
and much discussion about Indian affairs took place in
Parliament.   It was determined to examine witnesses at the
bar of the Commons; and Hastings was ordered to attend.
He had appeared at that bar once before.   It was when he 10
read his answer to the charges which Burke had laid on the
table.   Since that time twenty-seven years had elapsed;
public feeling had undergone a complete change; the nation
had now forgotten his faults, and remembered only his
services.   The reappearance, too, of a man who had been 15
among the most distinguished of a generation that had
passed away, who now belonged to history, and who seemed
to have risen from the dead, could not but produce a
solemn and pathetic effect.   The Commons received him
with acclamations, ordered a chair to be set for him, and 20
when he retired, rose and uncovered.   There were, indeed,
a few who did not sympathise with the general feeling.
One or two of the managers of the impeachment were
present.   They sate in the same seats which they had
occupied when they had been thanked for the services 25
which they had rendered in Westminster Hall: for, by the
courtesy of the House, a member who has been thanked in
his place is considered as having a right always to occupy
that place.   These gentlemen were not disposed to admit
that they had employed several of the best years of their 30
lives in persecuting an innocent man.   They accordingly
kept their seats, and pulled their hats over their brows; but
the exceptions only made the prevailing enthusiasm more

remarkable. The Lords received the old man with similar
tokens of respect. The University of Oxford conferred on
him the degree of Doctor of Laws; and, in the Sheldonian
Theatre, the undergraduates welcomed him with tumultuous
5 cheering.

These marks of public esteem were soon followed by
marks of royal favour. Hastings was sworn of the Privy
Council, and was admitted to a long private audience of
the Prince Regent, who treated him very graciously. When
10 the Emperor of Russia and the King of Prussia visited
England, Hastings appeared in their train both at Oxford
and in the Guildhall of London, and, though surrounded
by a crowd of princes and great warriors, was everywhere
received by the public with marks of respect and admiration.
15 He was presented by the Prince Regent both to Alexander
and to Frederic William; and his Royal Highness went so
far as to declare in public that honours far higher than a seat
in the Privy Council were due, and would soon be paid,
to the man who had saved the British dominions in Asia.
20 Hastings now confidently expected a peerage; but, from
some unexplained cause, he was again disappointed.

He lived about four years longer, in the enjoyment of
good spirits, of faculties not impaired to any painful or
degrading extent, and of health such as is rarely enjoyed
25 by those who attain such an age. At length, on the twenty-
second of August, 1818, in the eighty-sixth year of his age,
he met death with the same tranquil and decorous fortitude
which he had opposed to all the trials of his various and
eventful life.

30   With all his faults,—and they were neither few nor small,
—only one cemetery was worthy to contain his remains. In
that temple of silence and reconciliation where the enmities
of twenty generations lie buried, in the Great Abbey which

has during many ages afforded a quiet resting-place to those
whose minds and bodies have been shattered by the conten-
tions of the Great Hall, the dust of the illustrious accused
should have mingled with the dust of the illustrious accusers.
This was not to be. Yet the place of interment was not 5
ill chosen. Behind the chancel of the parish church of
Daylesford, in earth which already held the bones of many
chiefs of the house of Hastings, was laid the coffin of the
greatest man who has ever borne that ancient and widely
extended name. On that very spot probably, fourscore 10
years before, the little Warren, meanly clad and scantily
fed, had played with the children of ploughmen. Even
then his young mind had revolved plans which might be
called romantic. Yet, however romantic, it is not likely
that they had been so strange as the truth. Not only had 15
the poor orphan retrieved the fallen fortunes of his line.
Not only had he repurchased the old lands, and rebuilt the
old dwelling. He had preserved and extended an empire.
He had founded a polity. He had administered government
and war with more than the capacity of Richelieu. He had 20
patronised learning with the judicious liberality of Cosmo.
He had been attacked by the most formidable combination
of enemies that ever sought the destruction of a single
victim ; and over that combination, after a struggle of ten
years, he had triumphed. He had at length gone down to 25
his grave in the fulness of age, in peace, after so many
troubles, in honour, after so much obloquy.

　　Those who look on his character without favour or malevolence will pronounce that, in the two great elements of
all social virtue, in respect for the rights of others, and in 30
sympathy for the sufferings of others, he was deficient. His
principles were somewhat lax. His heart was somewhat
hard. But while we cannot with truth describe him either

as a righteous or as a merciful ruler, we cannot regard
without admiration the amplitude and fertility of his intellect, his rare talents for command, for administration,
and for controversy, his dauntless courage, his honourable
5 poverty, his fervent zeal for the interests of the state, his
noble equanimity, tried by both extremes of fortune, and
never disturbed by either.

NOTES.

PAGE 1.

Warren Hastings. This essay appeared in the *Edinburgh Review* in Oct. 1841, the volumes which it reviews having appeared in the same year. Some alterations were made subsequently. The text here followed is that of the collected essays published in 1850.

4. **Mr Gleig**, author of the *Life of Warren Hastings* of which this essay is a review. Gleig was born in 1796, served in the Peninsula and in the Washington campaign, and afterwards took orders in 1822. He died in 1888. He was author of many other works, of which the most notable was his *Life of the Great Duke of Wellington*.

18. **Goldsmith.** The author of *The Vicar of Wakefield, She Stoops to Conquer*, and *The Deserted Village*, was obliged to do much hack-work for booksellers (like his friend Samuel Johnson), and wrote among other things a very inefficient history of England. **Scott's** *Life of Napoleon* similarly was a piece of work wholly unworthy of the author's genius.

PAGE 2.

5. **the Prince of Machiavelli:** the treatise *Del Principe*, which might be called an essay on king-craft, by Nicolo Machiavelli, a Florentine statesman and man of letters. The work in question discusses the principles which should guide an autocrat, setting moral considerations entirely aside. It is a sort of essay on political iniquity viewed as a fine art. See Macaulay's *Essay on Machiavelli*.

6. **the Whole Duty of Man;** a highly didactic moral work attributed to Richard Allestre.

10. **Furor Biographicus,** "biographer's madness," a blind unreasoning enthusiasm for the person of whom the author writes—a disease as it were bred almost inevitably by his occupation.

31. **Mr Mill.** James Mill, father of John Stuart Mill, and author of a history of India. Mill's "severity" might in many cases, notably those of Hastings and Clive, be described rather as wilful injustice.

PAGE 3.

3. **Lely**: Sir Peter Lely, born in Westphalia in 1617, came to England in 1641 and rapidly became one of the favourite painters of the day. The favour in which he was held remained unaffected by the changes of government from Monarchy to a Republic, and from a Republic back to Monarchy. He was patronised by Charles I., painted Cromwell, and became state painter to Charles II.

17. **ancient and illustrious**: Burke, misled probably by Francis, curiously enough taunted Hastings with being of obscure origin.

19. **the...Danish sea-king**, by name Hasting.

23. **fable**; the legend of descent from Hasting cannot be proved, though it may be true.

24. **One branch...historians.** The name of Hastings is of frequent occurrence in Shakespeare's historical plays—in 2 *Henry IV.*, 3 *Henry VI.*, and *Richard III.* Laurence Hastings was made Earl of Pembroke by Edward III.; the Lord Hastings of Henry IV.'s reign took part in the Archbishop of York's rising; **the renowned Chamberlain,** William, Lord Hastings, was an adherent of Edward IV., and was brought to the block by Richard.

30. **was regained**; the earldom of Huntingdon became dormant in 1789 with the death of the earl. It was not till some thirty years later that Hans Francis Hastings established his claim to the peerage.

32. **Daylesford**, i.e. Hastings of Daylesford claimed to belong to an older branch of the Hastings family than the kinsmen who had been ennobled.

PAGE 4.

7. **the mint at Oxford.** London being held by the Parliament, Oxford became the head-quarters of Charles I., whose supporters sent quantities of gold and silver plate thither to be transformed into coin.

10. **Speaker Lenthal**, who presided at the trial of Charles I.

23. **Pynaston** or Penyston Hastings was twenty-six, not sixteen, when he married.

27. **was born.** It is uncertain whether this event took place at his father's house at Churchill in Oxfordshire or at the Daylesford rectory which is not many miles distant.

PAGE 5.

12. Isis, the river which flows past Oxford.

30. Newington, in Kent.

PAGE 6.

1. Vinny Bourne; Vincent Bourne, chiefly remarkable for his skill in writing Latin poems.

2. Churchill (Charles), a celebrated satirist, whose best known work is the *Rosciad*.

Colman (George), a well-known man of letters and dramatist.

3. Lloyd (Robert) was known as a poet, and Richard **Cumberland** as a dramatist.

4. Cowper (William), the only one of these contemporaries of Hastings who attained a really high literary position. His Muse was gentle and religious; but he was an undoubted poet.

15. the Ouse at Olney, where he lived with the Unwins and wrote most of his poems; of which the two most universally familiar are probably *The Task* and *John Gilpin*.

22. the doctrine of human depravity, i.e. that we are "altogether born in sin"—that the natural man left to his own devices, prefers evil to good. The Calvinistic school of theology to which Cowper belonged laid great stress on this doctrine, which was to a great extent responsible for the fits of religious depression and even insanity to which he was subject, as Bunyan had been before him.

29. Impey. Throughout this essay, Macaulay loses no opportunity of girding at Impey as a man who loved mischief much for its own sake and more for the sake of a bribe. There are three leading occasions in respect of which his character is impugned, but in none of the three can the charges brought by Macaulay be fairly maintained. These are (1) the Nuncomar affair (Intr. II. § 5, and pp. 44—48, notes), (2) the compromise of the quarrel between the Council and the Courts (Intr. II. § 5 *sub fin.* and p. 65, note) and (3) the collecting of affidavits in the affair of the Oude Begums (p. 88, note). This aspersion of Impey's character at Westminster is a flight of imagination; and in any case Impey would hardly have been "hired as fag" to a boy in his own form as Hastings was.

PAGE 7.

3. for the foundation; i.e. for a "foundation" scholarship.

6. studentship; at Christ Church, Oxford, what are called fellowships at other colleges are known as "studentships"; and the holder of a scholarship is termed a "junior student."

W. H.   10

19. writership : the junior clerks in the service of the Honourable East India Company in India were termed " writers."

28. October following : i.e. in October 1750. The ensuing paragraph is somewhat misleading in the matter of dates. In the war between French and English in India which was terminated in 1749 by the news of the Peace of Aix-la-Chapelle in 1748, the French had decidedly got the best of it. In 1749 began a struggle for the thrones of the Nizam of the Deccan and the Nawab of the Carnatic, in which the French supported Mirzapha Jung and Chunda Sahib, while the British supported Nazir Jung and Anwar-ud-din. In 1750 the two French candidates were *de facto* monarchs, the rival claimants were dead and Mahommed Ali, representing Anwar-ud-din's claim, was shut up in Trichinopoly. It was not till 1751 that Clive distinguished himself by the capture and defence of Arcot. (Intr. II. § 1, p. x.)

30. Calcutta, otherwise called Fort William, was the chief British factory in Bengal. The fighting between the English and French Companies had hitherto been confined to the Carnatic or Madras district.

33. the servants : notably Saunders, the governor of Madras, and Clive—though it is premature at this point to say that he had been transformed into a general.

PAGE 8.

1. the war of the succession : i.e. the war between the rival claimants to the thrones of the Nizam and the Nawab of the Carnatic.

2. the tide was as a matter of fact turned by the capture and defence of Arcot in 1751.

12. the prince : the Nawab of Bengal. The reigning Nawab, when Hastings arrived, was an able ruler known as Aliverdy Khan, who was shortly after succeeded by his son, the infamous Surajah Dowlah.

25. declared war : Surajah Dowlah had a general idea that he could get more money out of the English by crushing them than by encouraging their trade. Also he was annoyed because the governor, Drake, began to fortify Fort William for fear of an attack from the French at Chandernagore.

29. the Dutch Company : the Dutch had a factory at Chinsurah, on the Hoogley, above Calcutta. See Map III.

32. the Black Hole. The story of this horrible outrage is vividly narrated by Macaulay in his essay on Clive. On the night of June 20th, 1756, one hundred and forty-six English men and women were driven together in a room where there was barely space to stand; with the result that before morning all but twenty-three were already dead.

PAGE 9.

4. **Hoogley,** one of the rivers of the Ganges Delta, on which Calcutta is situated.

9. **The treason:** a plot was on foot to overthrow Surajah Dowlah and make his chief captain, Meer Jaffier, Nawab in his place. The other heads of the conspiracy were Jugget Seit and Roydullub, but many of the nobility were involved in it. When Clive's punitive expedition arrived from Madras the British took active part in the conspiracy, utilising it to overthrow Surajah Dowlah and substitute a Nawab who should be a puppet of their own.

25. **Plassey:** Clive marched against Surajah Dowlah and dispersed his army at this famous battle (June 23, 1757); and Meer Jaffier was made Nawab. Surajah Dowlah, falling into the hands of his enemies, was murdered. At Plassey, Clive's army numbered three thousand, of whom only one thousand were British. The Nawab's army numbered sixty thousand, but a great part of them were drawn off by Meer Jaffier during the battle.

30. **member of Council.** In each of the three presidencies (as they were afterwards called) of Bengal, Madras and Bombay, the affairs of the East India Company were managed by a Governor and Council. When Hastings was appointed to the Council, it was of course necessary for him to give up his post as Resident at Moorshedabad.

31. **the interval.** Clive left Bengal in 1760 and returned in 1765. The British, suddenly turned into irresistible masters where up till 1757 they had been mere tenants of the Nawab without any political power, used their new position entirely as a means to personal enrichment. Until Clive returned and reorganised affairs with a strong hand (Intr. II. § 1, *sub fin.*) there was a period of oppression and misgovernment without parallel in the history of British colonisation.

PAGE 10.

25. **dæmons:** supernatural Powers, demi-gods (δαίμονες); not "fiends," a sense which came from the mediaeval idea that the gods of the pagan world were devils.

PAGE 11.

5. **rotten boroughs.** At this time there were a large number of boroughs (each returning a member to Parliament) having only a very few voters, generally under the control of some local magnate. People who wished to enter Parliament cultivated—by bribery or otherwise—the good will of these magnates or of the voters themselves;

so that practically a large number of these seats were actually purchased. The rotten boroughs were particularly numerous in Cornwall. One of the objects of the great Reform Bill of 1832 was the abolition of these boroughs. There are numerous references to the subject in Macaulay's essay on Lord Clive, who in 1754 was a candidate for the Cornish borough of St Michael.

32. **buccaneer**: the name given to the rovers who infested the Spanish Main : and so extended to sea-rovers whose object was plunder. Newspapers now not uncommonly apply the term "buccaneering" to all sorts of expeditions which aim at obtaining booty by force of arms. The word is derived from French *boucaner*, to dry meat on a barbecue; having been first applied to the French hunters of St Domingo.

PAGE 12.

2. **unscrupulous** : even this term is perhaps stronger than the facts seem to warrant. Hastings as a politician was certainly not tender-hearted, and on particular occasions he was responsible for excessive severity ; but it is at least open to question whether he was ever deliberately unjust, and he was certainly never dishonest.

4. **1764**: thus Hastings himself was away from India during the whole of Clive's final administration, which lasted from 1765 to 1767.

PAGE 13.

1. **Hafiz** and **Ferdusi**: two Persian poets.

26. **a baron.** Imhoff's title appears to have been perfectly legitimate. His father was a Baron Christopher Imhoff, and traced descent duly from a crusading warrior.

29. **pagoda**: properly a Hindoo temple with its precincts ; but applied also as here to a gold coin.

32. **Archangel**: a port on the north coast of Russia. It is icebound for the greater part of the year.

PAGE 14.

8. **an Indiaman**: it must be remembered that the voyage to India round the Cape in a sailing vessel meant being associated with the same people every day and all day for six months—possibly less, probably more.

PAGE 15.

13. **Franconia**, in Saxony.

PAGE 16.

9. **Fort St George**: the alternative title for Madras, applied to the English quarter.

PAGE 17.

2. **Augustulus**: Romulus Augustulus was set on the throne of the Western Roman Empire by Orestes and Odoacer, A.D. 475; but in the following year Odoacer put Orestes to death and dethroned Augustulus.

Odoacer, the Herulian, having served in the army of the Western Empire assisted in making Romulus Augustus Emperor. Having dethroned Romulus, Odoacer acknowledged the authority of the Eastern Emperor Zeno at Byzantium, much as the British acknowledged the Mogul, keeping all power in his own hands. He governed with ability and success; until in 489 Theodoric the Ostrogoth invaded Italy and overthrew him, though he maintained himself in Ravenna till 493, when he was assassinated.

3. **Charles Martel and Pepin**, the grandfather and father of Charlemagne, were Mayors of the Palace to the Frankish kings of the Merovingian dynasty; holding all real power in their own hands. Pepin finally dethroned the last Childeric, and founded the Carlovingian dynasty. Macaulay dwells on this analogy at some length in his essay on Clive.

7. **writer or cadet**, the juniors in the Company's service, mercantile or military.

11. **At present**: when Macaulay wrote, the government of India was still in the hands of the East India Company; from which it was transferred to the Crown in 1858 after the great Mutiny.

12. **executive**, as distinguished from legislation and judicial administration.

19. **by Mr Pitt**, by the India Bill of 1784. When Warren Hastings went to Bengal in 1772, the system of government was that established by Clive. This was reconstructed by North's Regulating Act of 1773. For the changes then introduced, see Intr. II. § 5: and § 7 for Pitt's India Bill.

PAGE 18.

5. **political**: i.e. the term which properly covers the whole field of politics, foreign and domestic, is restricted in the Indian usage to the special branch of foreign affairs.

21. **The collection of the revenue, etc.**: i.e. in accepting the Diwanee (see Intr. II. § 1 *sub fin.*) the Company made themselves responsible for the Revenue affairs, but placed the administration of them not in the hands of the Company's English servants but of a native.

PAGE 19.

8. **Maharajah Nuncomar.** Nuncomar, otherwise called Nand Kumar or Nanda Kumar, was a Brahmin but not of the highest caste: nor had he inherited his title of Maharajah.

31. **the Ionian**: the Greeks are described by Juvenal as utterly effeminate and exceedingly clever. The lines are to be found in the Third Satire, 60—78.

> Non possum ferre, Quirites,
> Graecam urbem...quem vis hominem secum attulit ad nos:
> Grammaticus rhetor geometres pictor aliptes
> Augur schoenobates medicus magus, omnia novit
> Graeculus esuriens: in caelum, iusseris, ibit.

PAGE 20.

5. **All those millions**: it must be borne in mind that this description applies only to the true Bengalee. Even in Upper Bengal the race becomes sturdier, and the Rajput tribes of Oude supply excellent troops. Many of the Mahommedans of Bengal are again a different race, descended chiefly from Pathan or Afghan invaders.

23. **Mucius** Scaevola; who, according to the old Roman tale, when Lars Porsenna was besieging the city, made his way into the Etruscan camp to kill the king. Being seized, and brought before Porsenna, he was threatened with torture; whereupon, he thrust his hand into a flame, and held it there till it was burned, to show what a Roman would endure.

24. **Algernon Sydney**, a favourite hero of the Republican Whigs in England at the end of the seventeenth century. The Rye House Plot in 1683 was made an excuse for attacking him on the charge of complicity in it. Although the evidence against him was a mere farce, Judge Jefferies condemned him; and the fortitude with which he met his death became proverbial.

29. **forged documents**: this is a practice painfully familiar to our magistrates in India. Forgery is so customary, that we hear of cases where fictitious debts have been claimed on the evidence of forged papers which were rebutted by the production of forged receipts.

PAGE 21.

32. **a poorer country**: there were immense stores of wealth in the form of hoarded gold and jewels in the possession of a few potentates, but the revenues depending on the products of industry were small, and the general population was miserably poor.

Page 22.

25. **at Moorshedabad**, at the time of Surajah Dowlah's fall.

Page 23.

15. **that memorable day.** In 1760, Shah Alum, son of the titular Mogul who was a prisoner in his own palace at Delhi, attempted to invade Bengal and laid siege to Patna. Clive marched to relieve the town, and Shah Alum's army was dispersed by Captain Knox.

Page 24.

13. **the inoffensive child**; this does not mean that Goordas was a child at this time.

31. **After a long hearing**: the whole of this passage gives the impression that Hastings arrested Mahommed Reza Khan with a merely political object; and set him free as soon as that was attained. He certainly *used* the arrest for the political object; but he had made it by the positive orders of the directors, and the investigation demanded was carried out with the utmost thoroughness and care. The Minister was honourably acquitted, but only when the evidence against him had broken down on every point. The suggestion conveyed, that arrest and trial were merely a pretext, is hardly a fair one.

Page 25.

19. **to get money.** There is no question at all that *one* of the objects of most importance to Hastings was, to obtain money for government. But it was no more the sole object of his diplomacy, i.e. his dealings with native rulers, than it was of the internal administration of Bengal. The need of money was perhaps the leading motive, but there were others as well.

24. **Teviotdale**; the motto is that of the Cranstouns. But there is no doubt that the border families in a general way acted on it.

32. **great wrongs**: each of the "great wrongs" is capable of being reduced to countenancing excessive severity on the part of his associates. Whenever Hastings demanded rupees from Nawabs or Rajahs, he had a tenable if disputable claim. But provided his claim was tenable, considerations of generosity or even of leniency did not weigh with him.

Page 27.

6. **the great Mogul**, now Shah Alum. Clive, after Munro's victory at Buxar, had agreed to pay tribute to the Mogul, and had ceded the

district of Allahabad and Corah on the border of Bengal and Oude to Shah Alum. This had been done for two reasons ; one, that Allahabad was a strong military position which it was of great importance to keep well defended in friendly hands ; the other, that Shah Alum could not establish himself at Delhi. But Shah Alum's subsequent action had entirely upset the whole object of the treaty. He made terms with the Mahrattas—the very enemy against whom it was most necessary to keep guard—and proposed to reestablish himself at Delhi with their assistance and to hand over Allahabad and Corah to them in return. Shah Alum had in effect broken the understood conditions of the treaty ; besides which his action had made tribute paid to him virtually tribute paid to the Mahrattas. That under those circumstances, the cession should have been cancelled, and the districts re-occupied by the British, was a measure of military necessity ; that the tribute should be refused was not unreasonable ; while the subsequent arrangements with the Oude Vizier suited his views and were advantageous to the British. That Hastings's government got substantial benefit out of the transaction does not prove it to have been an act of unscrupulous rapacity.

20. **still governed**, until 1856. The annexation of Oude by Lord Dalhousie was one of the exciting causes of the Mutiny in 1857.

25. **impiety**: the sovereignty of the Mogul rested in part on his authority as the religious Head of the Indian Mussulmans.

29. **the Electors**: the title given to those Princes of the " Holy Roman Empire " who had a voice in the election of the Emperor. It must be remembered that the " Emperor" who plays so large a part in Mediaeval and Modern history till the end of the last century, was not (as he is frequently styled) ''the German Emperor " but nominally the successor of the Roman Emperors ; and that the office continued to be nominally elective, though in effect it became hereditary with the Austrian house of Habsburg.

PAGE **28.**

4. **torn from the Mogul**, see note on "the Great Mogul," p. 27.

17. **the passes** of the Himalayas.

20. **Hyphasis and Hystaspes** or Hydaspes : the Greek names for two of the five great rivers which flow through the Punjab. They are identified with the Beas and the Jhelum.

26. **Ghizni** or Guzni, a fortress in Afghanistan, captured by Sir J. Keane in the Afghan campaign of 1839.

PAGE **29.**

1. **Rohillas** : this name signifies " mountaineers."

2. **fiefs of the spear**, lands held for military service.

4. **that fertile plain**, on the N.W. of Oude.

6. **Aurungzebe** died in 1707. It took the Rohillas another forty years to establish themselves as masters of the Hindoo population of Rohilcund. (Intr. II. § 4.)

10. **honourably distinguished**: the government of Rohilcund at this time was in the hands of Hafiz Rahmat, who was a good ruler and soldier. As the Rohillas themselves were restrained, and their fighting reputation kept them fairly free from attack, Rohilcund did for the time enjoy a season of prosperity. But the Rohilla system and the Rohilla character did not differ materially from those of other Pathan conquerors. Good government depended mainly on the continued control of one particular man.

19. **Right, or show of right**: in the first place, Sujah Dowlah believed that the Rohillas were intriguing with the Mahrattas for a descent on Oude: in the second, they had not carried out their pledges to repay him for help rendered when the Mahrattas had threatened Rohilcund: and in the third, a race which has established itself for less than half a century in a given territory by aggressive conquest can hardly protest against the injustice of being turned out again by conquest. In short, Sujah Dowlah had about as much right in Rohilcund as the Rohillas themselves.

21. **Catherine** of Russia, who in 1773 was joined by Prussia and Austria in the partition of Poland for their common convenience.

the Bonaparte family. Napoleon made his brother Joseph king of Spain, in 1808.

31. **many fields of battle**: notably in the great battle of Paniput in 1761, when they helped Ahmed Shah to defeat the Mahrattas.

32. **eighty thousand**: there were probably never more than 40,000 of the Rohillas: and they numbered only about one-twentieth of the inhabitants of Rohilcund. To the enormous mass of the population it was a matter of indifference whether Rohillas or the Oude Vizier should rule over them; except so far as the Rohillas may be held to have shown signs of superiority to the other Mussulman races.

PAGE 30.

2. **one army**: the Rohillas themselves seem to have been doubtful of their capacity for resisting the Mahrattas.

28. **infamous.** Throughout this paragraph, Macaulay begs the whole question. If to dispossess the Rohillas was wicked, to help in dispossessing them for the sake of money was wicked also. But if the dispossession was justifiable, the help was justifiable.

32. **The object was a great deal more.** It was to eject from their

position as over-lords of Rohilcund a race whose presence was felt to be a menace to Oude. The money may have served as an inducement to overrate the danger from the Rohillas; but there is no doubt that the danger was regarded as genuine and serious.

PAGE 31.

25. caput lupinum: a "wolf's head" or outlaw, one to whom no law extends protection.

PAGE 32.

2. offered a large ransom: they did not however undertake to pay even the sums admittedly due under treaty to the Vizier.

7. The dastardly sovereign, etc. There appears to be no authority for this statement. It may also be remarked that there were twice as many of the Oude troops killed as of Champion's brigade.

22. fled from their homes: this refers to the Hindoo population, who did not wait to see whether they would be subjected to violence. The fact that an invading army was on the way was sufficient.

27. Champion remonstrated, and from his dispatches it appears that the remonstrances had a very marked effect. But the most ingenious defence cannot cover the fact that Hastings ought to have made express stipulations beforehand, instead of merely trusting to the influence of Champion in checking the excesses of an army over which he had no actual authority.

PAGE 34.

18. Lord North came into office in 1770. The Regulating Acts were passed in 1773. See Intr. II. § 5.

PAGE 35.

17. the Letters of Junius, a series of letters addressed to public men, remarkable for brilliant and merciless invective. The authorship has been attributed to various persons, but the balance of opinion undoubtedly assigns it to Francis, though the problem will probably never be solved beyond doubt.

PAGE 37.

11. Woodfall, the printer of the letters.

19. the Hebrew prophet: Jonah.

30. Old Sarum: a flagrant instance of a "rotten borough." A single voter returned the member; while such great manufacturing towns as Manchester and Leeds were unrepresented.

PAGE 38.

7. **George Grenville,** leader of the "Bedford" section of the Whigs, and primarily responsible for the legislation which was the direct cause of the breach with the American colonies.

10. **the Middlesex election.** John Wilkes had been elected Member of Parliament for Middlesex; but the House, which decided election petitions in those days, declared the election void on the ground of his previous expulsion. He was twice re-elected and unseated in the same way, amidst the wildest popular excitement.

PAGE 39.

26. **Bombay:** the authorities at Bombay were the originators of the trouble. Ragoba (see Intr. II. § 3) claimed the office of Peshwa, and the Bombay government agreed to support his claim, Salsette and Bassein being ceded to them in return. They displayed an unfailing capacity for blundering throughout the subsequent operations: while the efforts of Hastings to repair mismanagement were seriously hampered by the determination of the majority of the Council to oppose every measure of which he approved.

PAGE 41.

7. **Oates, Bedloe,** and **Dangerfield** were the principal informers in the famous "Popish Plot" of 1678. The "plot" had no existence and the "information" was a tissue of falsehoods, the whole thing having been concocted partly for pay and partly to procure the ruin of a few individuals.

PAGE 42.

3. **a proper place.** The point of Hastings's argument was, that in no case was the Council a proper tribunal for trying charges against the Governor-General: least of all when a majority of members were openly and obviously violently biassed against him. But he offered to have a special committee of enquiry appointed.

PAGE 43.

7. **higher authority,** i.e. the Court of Directors.

PAGE 44.

5. **possessing himself.** This phrase implies that Hastings had taken measures to make sure that the judges would be on his side. There is no evidence of anything of the kind. He and Impey were

on the best of terms personally; but there was no impropriety or "managing" implied in that.

15. the opinion of every body has changed since Macaulay's day. Probably the majority of candid enquirers now believe that Hastings was not the mover in the matter. The charge itself was genuine and natural ; and the only evidence against Hastings is that it happened to be brought at an opportune moment for him—which is clearly no real evidence at all.

26. before Sir Elijah Impey: as a matter of fact the case was brought before the *four* judges, Sir Elijah presiding. See Intr. II. § 5.

32. so strangely ignorant. Macaulay misses the point. The judges alone could grant a respite ; but the Council might have recommended a reprieve till the matter could be referred home. Since the majority considered the question and expressly declined to make any such recommendation, they recognised that there was no sufficient reason for taking an exceptional course—certainly no "clear case" for a respite. Had the recommendation been made and set on one side by Impey, the case against him would no doubt wear the aspect which Macaulay seeks to put upon it.

PAGE 45.

11. Impey and his brother judges were agreed that the law as they had laid it down should take its course. There was nothing exceptional about the procedure one way or other.

PAGE 46.

16. a Brahmin, etc. This is a highly exaggerated picture. Nuncomar was a Brahmin, but not of the highest order. Brahmins are not few and far between in Benga', and the country had been governed for a couple of centuries by Mussulmans to whom Brahmins were of no more account than their neighbours. For a Brahmin to be put to death was in no way an unparalleled shock to the Hindoo mind. Nuncomar was not even the first Brahmin who had been sentenced to death for forgery, though in the previous case the sentence had been commuted on petition. But the execution of such a man as Nuncomar for such a crime as forgery was no doubt a very great shock.

PAGE 48.

13. Dacca, a large town in lower Bengal.

17. No rational man: legal opinion to-day however, as well as that of Impey's three fellow-judges, confirms the view that the trial was fairly and impartially conducted, the verdict sound, and the sentence correct.

22. "**to whose support,**" etc. (1) It may at least be plausibly held that these words refer to a quite different occasion, when the Supreme Court upheld Hastings at the time of Clavering's attempt to claim the Governor-Generalship, as narrated on p. 55. (2) If they refer to the Nuncomar affair at all, they imply nothing more than that Impey refused to be intimidated by the clamour of Hastings's enemies— a resolution for which he did in fact subsequently suffer.

Page 49.

17. Lord Stafford : one of the victims in the " Popish Plot " affair. See note on Oates, p. 41.

Page 51.

1. Dr Johnson : cf. p. 13, where the fact of a correspondence is referred to.

6. Tour to the Hebrides. Johnson had published an account of his tour to the Hebrides in 1773. In 1774 he sent Hastings a copy, having already written to him that year a letter accompanying a present of Sir William Jones's Persian Grammar, published in 1771. The date of Nuncomar's condemnation was June 16, 1775.

Page 52.

20. Macleane's action certainly does not seem warranted by the instructions ; which were, that he was to give in the resignation if there was "an evident disinclination" towards Hastings. This was certainly not covered by a majority of a hundred votes in his favour.

Page 53.

15. He began to revolve : as pointed out in Intr. II. § 3, this statement is not a correct account of the Governor-General's policy. Hastings wished to strengthen the position in Bengal, but not to extend territory.

18. subsidiary alliances ; i.e. alliances by which the native states should subsidise the Company's troops for their own security, thus at the same time enabling the Company to exercise an effective control over their policy.

20. Berar: a province lying between the Deccan and Bengal. The special reference here is to the Mahratta "Bhonsla" of Nagpore.

Page 55.

1. The court pronounced : it is at least possible that this is the act to which Hastings referred in the words which Macaulay applied unhesitatingly to the Nuncomar affair (see p. 48 and note)—"The man to whose support he was at one time indebted for the safety of his fortune, honour, and reputation."

32. the...dangers: the fortunes of the American war had turned; Burgoyne had surrendered at Saratoga, and France had declared war in support of the colonists. Spain joined France in June 1779; war was declared against Holland in Dec., 1780, after the whole of the Baltic powers had joined in the Armed Neutrality, a naval combination to resist the right claimed by the British of searching neutral vessels for contraband of war.

PAGE 56.

15. which had guided: the reference is to William Pitt, afterwards Lord Chatham. Until power came into his hands, vigour and genius had been conspicuously absent from George II.'s councils.

20. Ireland was demanding redress of grievances, and the "Volunteer movement" under which numbers of the population had taken up arms—not against England, but because the troops in Ireland were insufficient to protect her in case of a French invasion—made the situation dangerous, from the fear that the Volunteers might follow the example of the American colonies.

24. Calpe: Gibraltar, which was besieged from July, 1779 to October, 1782: during which time the British twice threw in reliefs.

the Mexican Sea: until Rodney's great victory of "The Saints" in April, 1782, the allied fleets at the West Indies were always larger than that of England.

25. the British Channel: in 1781 the French and Spanish fleets appeared in the Channel with 50 ships of the line, while the English Admiral had only 30 to oppose to them. They did not, however, venture on an engagement.

30. An attack by sea: in 1782 however, Suffren appeared in Indian waters, and gradually gained the ascendency there.

31. The danger was: a certain French adventurer, the Chevalier St Lubin, in 1777 entered on negotiations with the Mahratta chiefs in the character of a French emissary.—From this passage, it would be easy to get the impression that a European ally could readily furnish troops to native powers. But there could be no such danger, unless the French gained command of the sea. It was proved clearly in the wars of 1745—1761 that while the British controlled the sea, the French could not for long be really formidable in India. The seriousness of the situation rose precisely from the risk of the allied European navies being able to gain control of Indian waters—as in fact happened for a very brief interval in 1782—3.

5. **Aurungzebe** died in 1707. He was the last conqueror among the Moguls.

6. **Sevajee.** Madha Rao Sivaji, who began to form the Mahrattas into a nation. See Introduction II. § 2, and the Map of Northern and Central India.

17. **Berar**: the Bonsla's head-quarters were at Nagpore.

19. **Scindia** or Sindiah and **Holkar** at Gwalior and Indore respectively; the Guicowar or Gaikwar, at Baroda. **Gooti** and **Tanjore** were not centres of Mahratta power; they were but offshoots.

28. **Tamerlane** or Timur the Tartar, ancestor of Baber, who founded the Mogul dynasty.

7. **French adventurer**: St Lubin. See note, supra, p. 56, line 31.

15. **a pretender**: Ragonath Rao, commonly called Ragoba. See Intr. II. § 3. Hastings did not apparently intend to attack the Mahrattas; but the Bombay government on their own responsibility supported Ragoba, and were seriously worsted in attempting to force him on the chiefs. In the face of the reverse, Hastings felt it impossible to withdraw from the contest.

12. **a new...danger** from Hyder Ali of Mysore.

26. **Lally** was sent to command the French in India in 1759. He was a brave and even brilliant soldier, but utterly wanting in tact. Hence he alienated the natives by disregarding their religious prejudices, quarrelled with all his officers, and brought his army to the verge of mutiny. Unsupported by the French government, he carried on a hopeless struggle; and the war was practically decided by Eyre Coote's victory at Wandewash.—Lally was the son of an Irish refugee. When he was restored to France from his captivity in England he was put to death by the French government—to their lasting disgrace.

9. **Porto Novo.** The battle at which Coote in July 1781 checked the career of Hyder Ali. **Pollilore** was a second victory over the same foe in the following August.

13. **two independent powers**: see Intr. II. § 5.

Page 62.

22. mesne process: a technical legal term: pronounced "mean." The word means "middle" or "intermediate." The effect was that a man might be arrested up country, some hundreds of miles from Calcutta, and be brought up thither and detained for trial. When the slowness of communication is considered, the enormous expense and injustice involved for an innocent man is obvious. The freedom with which false accusations were brought rendered the process trebly unjust.

26. **an oath**; there seems to be no ground for this statement.

31. **To these outrages**; as far as concerns violation of the privacy of zenanas (the women's quarters of the household) this appears to be at any rate an exaggeration.

Page 63.

10. **Wat Tyler** headed an insurrection in the reign of Richard II. A poll-tax—i.e. a tax of so much for every member of the family—was levied, which the common people could only pay with extreme difficulty. When one of the tax-collectors insulted Wat Tyler's daughter, the population rose and marched on London, demanding redress. There, however, Sir William Walworth broke Wat Tyler's head with his mace, and the young king announced to the insurgents that *he* would be their leader and remedy their grievances—a promise which he neglected to keep.

25. **barrators**: a technical legal term for one who maliciously incites to litigation.

28. **spunging-houses**: in former times, when a man was arrested for debt he was taken to the "spunging-house," i.e. the house of a sheriff's officer, and was there confined until the trial. Here he had to pay for every pretence of comfort, at the most exorbitant rates, till he was "squeezed dry like a spunge": hence the term.

Page 64.

1. **There were instances.** Sir James Stephen, in the "Story of Nuncomar," reduces these to one case of a man who died while being conveyed from Dacca to Calcutta after judgment had gone against him: one known case and one reported of zenanas being entered: besides the case referred to in the next note but one.

3. **alguazils**: a Spanish term for bailiffs; being a corruption of the Moorish Al wazir, or minister.

10. **defending, sword in hand**: there was one occasion when a Mahommedan was afraid that a zenana would be broken into. He stood before the door, sword in hand; no attempt was made on it;

but a scuffle taking place in the house, he went and joined in, and was hurt.

14. **No Mahratta invasion**—invasions not infrequently accompanied by wholesale massacres and mutilations. It would be less unreasonable to compare the "horrors" of an English gaol at the same date with those of the Black Hole of Calcutta.

PAGE 65.

15. **were served with writs**: this gives a wholly false impression. Neither Impey nor the Supreme Court issued writs on their own account: but Cossinauth, plaintiff in an action against the Rajah of Cossijurah, demanded writs against Hastings and the Members of Council for preventing him by armed force from compelling the Rajah's attendance.

18. **set at liberty**: Hastings set no one at liberty.

25. **a bribe**: this is a curious perversion. The Governor and Council had the sanction of military force: the Courts had no possible means of resistance; if writs were issued they could not be enforced. The whole machinery was brought absolutely to a stand-still. After nine months of deadlock, Hastings proposed to give the Courts the sanction of the Council's support—so setting the machinery at work again—on condition that in certain departments the Chief Justice should accept the position of a servant of the Company: in respect of which departments he should receive emoluments from the Company. It might conceivably be urged that Impey should have refused the additional emoluments; but had he done so—had he remained in a position in which he had nothing to lose by resisting the Council—it would at once have been urged that there was no security against his bringing on a deadlock again whenever he was so minded. There is no shadow of evidence that Impey had fought the Council with the object of getting an increase of pay. The plain fact was, that the position of the Supreme Court, while in opposition to the Council and consequently unable to enforce its jurisdiction, was hopelessly anomalous. But the anomaly could only be removed by the Justices consenting to act as the servants of the Company; and the proposal that they should do so could only come from the Council; because, coming from the Judges, it would necessarily have been tantamount to a demand for pay as the Company's servants, as a condition.

PAGE 66.

9. **Jefferies**, more correctly Jeffreys; the judge who held the "Bloody Assize" after Monmouth's rebellion, in the reign of James II.,

and who throughout his career on the bench, from the days of the Rye House Plot till the coming of William of Orange, was infamous for his flagrant disregard of every element of justice.

26. **powers which,** etc.; but Impey's position was that he was entitled to the powers in question but was prevented from exercising them. He never abdicated them. He simply accepted the terms on which he would be *allowed* to enforce them up to a certain point. Moreover, he accepted them with the express provision that they should be referred to London for sanction. But see Intr. II. § 5.

Page 67.

31. **They met, and fired**: the distance was fourteen paces, which Hastings considered an unnecessarily long distance.

Page 68.

21. **a Mahommedan soldier**: Hyder Ali of Mysore.

Page 69.

3. **Louis the Eleventh,** the French king who consolidated France by systematically breaking down the power of the great vassals, who until his day had been able to dispute the authority of the crown and virtually to wage war as independent princes. "Every schoolboy knows" the portrait of him given in Scott's *Quentin Durward*.

13. **the most formidable enemy**: a noteworthy mark of his exceptional capacity is observable in the fact that he realised the immense strategic value that a French fleet might have in Indian waters, and negotiated accordingly with the French Commandant at Mauritius.—It is however scarcely true that he was more formidable than the Mahrattas became later. It was not till some four years after this Essay was written that the British fought the Sikhs, who were the finest troops we ever conquered on Indian soil.

18. **provoked,** etc.: the Madras authorities in the first place annoyed Hyder Ali by not supporting him in a quarrel with the Nizam, and went on later to irritate him by marching troops across his territory and seizing the French port of Mahé though he had declared it under his protection. Hyder Ali's invasion has been painted in one of Edmund Burke's finest descriptions.

31. **the Coleroon** or Kalrun is a river descending from the Mysore Hills and crossing the Carnatic. It falls into the sea just south of Porto Novo. (See Map of the Carnatic.)

33. **Mount St Thomas**, close to Madras. For the expression here cf. Macaulay's *Horatius*:

> "Now, from the rock Tarpeian,
> Could the wan burghers spy
> The line of blazing villages
> Red in the midnight sky."

PAGE 70.

13. **Munro**: the victor of Buxar in 1765.
29. **Coromandel**: i.e. the Carnatic.

PAGE 71.

1. **monsoon**: the monsoon is a wind which occurs annually at the same period. In summer it blows from the south-west, in winter from the north-east.

PAGE 72.

14. **Benares** on the Ganges. See Map III.
19. **oriels**: i.e. oriel windows: used loosely for any windows built out, so as to overhang. The origin of the name is doubtful. Skeat says it is *aureolum*, i.e. "a gilded chamber."

PAGE 73.

3. **Petit Trianon**: in some editions, **"Versailles"** is substituted. The "petit Trianon" was a château built by Louis XV. for Madame Du Barry. There was also a "grand Trianon," built by Louis XIV. for Madame de Maintenon.
5. **Golconda** in the Nizam's dominions. Diamonds and other jewels from the mines in the Deccan were brought to Golconda for cutting and setting, so that it became the great mart for precious stones.
9. **lords of Benares**: this is a curious account of the matter. The "lords" of Benares were simply great landowners. The Nawab of Oude bestowed the title of "Rajah" on Bulwunt Singh; and in the course of general political arrangements Bulwunt Singh became a tributary of the British instead of Oude. Cheyte Singh was the son of Bulwunt Singh.

PAGE 74.

14. **Hugh Capet**; the "Duke of Paris," whose son was the first king of that dynasty which continued as the house of Capet—of Valois—of Navarre—of Bourbon—until the fall of Louis Philippe: supplanting the last of the Carlovingians or Karlings.

11—2

16. **constitutional right** means a right established either by statute or by fully recognised custom. But in India there were no rights fully established by custom among the ruling classes, for the simple reason that no ruling class had been long enough established for other rights than those of the strong hand to be fully recognised. It is only under a long established and consistent government that "constitutional" rights come into existence.

21. **Charles the Tenth** came to the throne of France in 1824. In July 1830 he issued three ordinances which were contrary to the Charter to which he had taken the oath of adherence on ascending the throne. The ordinances therefore were in excess of the powers which the established laws allowed to the monarch. As a result, he was obliged to abdicate within a fortnight : being succeeded by Louis Philippe.

24. **Louis Bonaparte,** afterwards Napoleon III., who attempted an insurrection to recover the crown of France some time before the celebrated "Coup d'État" which established him as Emperor.

PAGE 75.

5. **the heir of Sevajee:** the descendant of the great Madha Rao Sivaji, who made a nation of the Mahrattas, was nominal sovereign at Poonah; but the office of Peshwa or first minister had become hereditary, and authority was vested not in the Rajah but in the Peshwa—even when the Peshwa was a baby, as he was at this time. Though the Peshwa was recognised as head of the Mahrattas, Scindia was the most powerful personality.

10. **a single government;** the Poonah Rajah and the Peshwa were neither of them really rulers of the Mahratta confederacy : the Mogul had no power, though he was *de jure* sovereign of half India : the British and the Nizam were *de facto* sovereigns, but both *de jure* subordinate to the Mogul : the Nawab of Oude was *de jure* subordinate to the Mogul, but *de facto* semi-subordinate to the British : the Nawab of the Carnatic was *de jure* subordinate to the Nizam, *de facto* to the British ; and Hyder Ali of Mysore was an adventurer who had created his own throne.

PAGE 77.

15. **intending to keep it;** the evidence that he never did so is fairly conclusive. He not only directed that it should be received by the sub-treasurer of the Council : but also sent information to the Directors in the same year ; and he transferred the money to the public accounts as soon as Francis left India.

29. **Hastings was determined,** etc: Macaulay omits to mention

that Cheyte Singh was gravely suspected of a design to throw off the
British supremacy altogether ; an idea which may very well have seemed
feasible in view of Hyder Ali's successes at this time (1780)—and of the
expectation that the French would be soon attacking the British in
India. The demand for a body of cavalry was also Coote's suggestion
and was approved by the Council.

PAGE 78.

14. **he began to think**, etc.: there seems to be no authority for
this statement.

PAGE 79.

14. **Bahar**: included in the Bengal dominion; but really a separate
province, lying between Oude and Bengal proper.

PAGE 81.

21. **Major Popham** had won the highest distinction by his brilliant
capture of Scindia's rock-fortress of Gwalior, which had been supposed
to be quite impregnable.

PAGE 84.

3. **been left in possession**: on the death of Sujah Dowlah, the
Begums claimed these estates and treasures. The majority of the Council
overruled Hastings, insisted on Asaph-ul-Dowlah allowing the claim,
and gave the Begums the Council's guarantee. It was now argued that
the guarantee was in its nature revocable, and that Hastings—having
from the beginning denied the Begum's claim—was entitled to act on
the view which he had always maintained. Further it was urged that
the Begums had encouraged the Benares disturbance, and having virtually supported rebellion were no longer entitled to consideration.

14. **had extorted**; i.e. he had extracted ready money from her;
but he had given her in return estates with a revenue which amply com-
pensated for the loan.

23. **shrank from them**: not on moral grounds, as the words suggest,
but because the Nawab was very much afraid of his exceedingly vigorous
mother and grandmother.

26. **plighted faith**: the whole question of "plighted faith" turns
on the nature of the guarantee. Was the guarantee given by the Council
revocable or not? i.e. was it merely a guarantee during the Council's
pleasure? This was a question fairly open to argument. Hastings held
that it was revocable at the Council's pleasure ; and that on the most
antagonistic interpretation, its validity was dependent on the good be-

haviour of the Begums, since all guarantees were necessarily given on that understanding whether expressed or not.

PAGE 85.

2. **Evidence for the imputation :** this is a matter of opinion. The English political officers resident in Benares positively affirmed that Cheyte Singh had been aided by troops in the pay of the Begums.

20. **implored**—more accurately, defied.

PAGE 86.

32. **infirm old men :** one of them at any rate was exceeding prosperous twenty years later.

PAGE 87.

26. **There is a man ; in** subsequent editions, Macaulay omitted this paragraph.

PAGE 88.

6. **an English soldier:** Mr Gleig served in the army before he took Orders as a clergyman.

11. **to do justice :** it would really be quite reasonable to read "injustice." In the first place Impey did not "intrude" himself; he was sent for by Hastings. The object of the enquiry, such as it was, was not to incriminate the Begums, but to obtain information relative to the Benares rising. In administering an affidavit, the officer is not concerned with the character of the information, or the sifting of its truth ; all he has to do is, to be sure that the deponent swears to the truth of the affidavit. Hence it was of no consequence whether Impey could or could not understand the contents of the affidavits. And finally, the evidence of the affidavits acquired no additional validity from the fact that the Chief Justice administered them, except on the general hypothesis that the deponents were less likely to commit perjury under the circumstances.

24. **Foot-note :** this note is Macaulay's own. It does not of course appear in the original " Edinburgh " article, but was added in consequence of the comments made thereon.

PAGE 89.

26. **Dundas:** the real author of Pitt's India Bill of 1784, afterwards Lord Melville.

18. **Secretary of State,** Lord Shelburne.

13. **thirteen colonies,** the thirteen American colonies which formed the United States.

15. **the right of legislating:** an Irish Parliament sat in Dublin till the Act of Union in 1801. But all its legislation was subject to the approval of the British Privy Council, so that its powers were to a very great extent nugatory. In 1783 the Irish Parliament was made for most purposes independent. This was the commencement of what is known as "Grattan's Parliament."

in the Mediterranean Minorca had been lost: in the **Gulf of Mexico** Florida: in **Africa** Senegal and Goree.

17. **the Dutch Deputies,** when Holland and England were fighting as allies in the War of the Spanish Succession, in the reign of Queen Anne.

19. **Mr Percival:** Prime Minister in England, when Wellington was conducting the Peninsular War.

12. **Adam Smith,** author of *The Wealth of Nations*, commonly called the Father of Political Economy.

17. **a more virtuous ruler;** Lord William Bentinck, who was Governor-General when Macaulay went out to India as a Member of Council: and who, with Macaulay's assistance, reconstructed the system of education in India.

28. **the Asiatic Society:** a Calcutta society for the encouragement of Oriental studies.

31. **Sir William Jones:** author of the Persian Grammar referred to in a previous passage (p. 51.)

33. **Pundits,** professional men of learning.

14. **The first English conquerors:** the reference is to the period of British misrule in Bengal during Clive's absence before 1765.

31. **a jingling ballad:** this is a curiously unfortunate illustration. The rhyme, as at present sung, sometimes has the name of Warren Hastings in it, sometimes that of Colonel Monson who was obliged to

beat an ignominiously hasty retreat before Holkar in 1804. In either case it implies a helter-skelter flight on the part of its hero—the Hastings version is supposed to refer to his retreat from Benares. Colonel Yule gives the lines—

Ghore par hauda, hāthī par jīn,

Jaldī bagh-gāyā ⎰Warren Hastīn!

⎱Kornail Munsīn!

i.e.   "Howdah on horse, saddle on elephant,

Quickly away bolted Warren Hastings."

The wrong arrangement of saddles and howdahs is of course part of the jest. It is likely enough that it is merely an adaptation of a much older jingle; but in any case it is about as complimentary to Hastings as "Malbrough s'en va-t-en guerre" to Marlborough..

PAGE 99.

3. **zemindar**, landholder.

6. **Carlton House**: the residence of George Prince of Wales, afterwards George IV.

9. **Mrs Hastings**: rumour seems to be the only ground for this charge. If Mr Gleig was a biographer of the type Macaulay would have us believe, he would certainly not have left the accusation unnoticed—he would have discovered a plausible justification.

26. **round-house**, the state cabin in the after part of the ship.

PAGE 100.

4. **Sir Charles Grandison**, the hero of Richardson's novel of that name; a gentleman whose morals, manners, and appearance were all unimpeachable. **Miss Byron** was the object of his dignified affections.

20. **Otium Divos**: Horace, *Odes* II. 16.

26. **his own conduct**: he was Governor-General from 1793—1798.

PAGE 101.

27. **Grattan**: the great Irish orator and statesman; one of the few whose name is honoured by men of every party.

PAGE 103.

12. **trunk-makers, etc.** were reputed to buy up printed waste-paper which could be turned to no other use.

24. **Lord Mansfield**, one of the greatest of English judges.

26. **Lord Lansdowne**, better known as Lord Shelburne. He had been a prominent politician for many years, and a supporter of Chatham. On the fall of North's administration, in March 1782, he and Charles

James Fox became the leading members of the second Rockingham administration. On Rockingham's death in June, Shelburne became Prime Minister; but early in 1783 he was driven out of office by the Coalition ministry of Fox and North; they again were expelled from office in December, and Pitt became Prime Minister. Pitt however would not have Shelburne in his Cabinet, and he was excluded from office but was made Marquis of Lansdowne.

28. **The ministers:** Pitt was returned to power with a sweeping majority after the dissolution of Parliament which took place in March 1784. The most active of Pitt's supporters was Dundas, afterwards Lord Melville.

31. **Fox's...Bill.** The Bill brought in by Fox and North, was carried in the Commons, but rejected by the Lords, the king using his personal influence to get it thrown out. It is certain however that the bill was unpopular. It had proposed that the powers of the Directors and Proprietors of the East India Company should be restricted entirely to matters of trade: that political powers should be vested in a body of seven commissioners appointed by Parliament, and holding office for four years; that the commercial arrangements should be in the hands of nine commissioners, selected by Parliament from among the Directors and Proprietors; and vacancies in these two bodies respectively were to be filled by appointment of the Crown and of the Proprietors. The popular objections were, that this was an interference with the rights of a chartered company; and would give the parliamentary majority for the time being effective control of all Indian appointments.

PAGE 104.

19. **censure,** which Dundas had moved, see p. 90. This was while Fox, Shelburne and Pitt were all nominally members of one party.

PAGE 105.

16. **the coalition** of Fox and North, which had overthrown Shelburne, and been in turn overthrown by Pitt.

20. **Brooks's:** the great Whig club to which Fox, Sheridan and many of the most brilliant wits of the day belonged.

PAGE 107.

10. **alienated:** Burke had belonged to the Rockingham section of the Whigs; Fox had headed the section whose views were somewhat more extreme. They remained united in the Fox and North coalition, at which time Shelburne and Pitt were favoured by the king; to whose political influence Fox and Burke were alike strongly opposed. The

return of Pitt to power was therefore a triumph for the king.   Later however, when the storm-cloud of the French Revolution burst over Europe, Fox in England represented the sympathisers with the new movement; but Burke's orderly and constitutional instincts were aroused, and he became an ardent opponent of the Revolution, and by consequence a supporter of the Crown; and his personal friendship with Fox was brought to an end.

19. **had committed**: Burke at any rate honestly believed so.

23. **Las Casas, 1474—1566.** A Spaniard who, as priest and bishop, devoted his life to the defence of the Indians of Mexico against the oppression of the Spaniards.

Clarkson, a Quaker, and a leading associate of Wilberforce in the crusade against the Slave-trade.

Page 108.

25. **imaum**: the Mussulman priest.

Mecca: the sacred city of the Mahommedans, who pray with their faces turned towards Mecca as the Jews in captivity with their faces towards Jerusalem.

26. **devotees swinging**: this refers to a curious form of religious fanaticism, in which the devotees of the goddess Kali were suspended in the air by hooks thrust through the flesh.

29. **yellow streaks**: marks on the forehead.

Page 109.

2. **Beaconsfield**: the residence of Burke in Buckinghamshire.

10. **Lord George Gordon**; a more or less insane nobleman who headed a "no popery" panic which was accompanied in 1780 by most serious riots in and round London and elsewhere. A graphic picture of these riots is given in *Barnaby Rudge.*

11. **Dr Dodd**; an eloquent divine, and a writer of considerable repute, who was hanged for forgery in 1777.

32. **the Stamp Act**; an Act passed by the British Parliament in 1765 for raising revenue from the American colonies. It became at once the formal ground for American declamation against unconstitutional legislation from London. Burke and the Rockingham Whigs opposed the measure, which was repealed by the first Rockingham administration in 1766.

Page 110.

7. **the Commercial Treaty**; of 1787—a step in the direction of Free Trade with France, taken by Pitt.—Fox and Burke opposed it,

generally on the ground that the natural hostility of France would induce
that country to use the treaty more with a view to injuring England
than to benefitting herself.

8. **the Regency:** in 1788, George III. having fallen a prey to insanity, there was a fierce contest as to the method of appointing a
Regent. Pitt maintained that the appointment rested with Parliament:
Fox and his followers declared that the same rule held good as in the
case of the king's death: since a regency bill, like any other, could not
become law until it received the royal assent; which it could not receive,
unless there was a legal representative of the Crown to give it. Therefore
they argued that if the king was incapacitated, the heir to the throne
must by that mere fact become the king's legal representative. The
theory was convenient for Fox, because the Prince of Wales was his
personal intimate. The debate was terminated by the king's restoration
to health.

the French Revolution; Burke's attitude to the French Revolution
was in the judgment of most historians wanting in insight into its causes;
but he did not misrepresent events in his denunciations of it, as he did
in his denunciations of Hastings.

24. **He should have felt:** had Hastings's acts been what Macaulay
represents, this would be true. But since he held that the worst of them
were not merely justified by political necessity but were morally defensible, he can hardly be reproached for maintaining his ground instead
of owning to misconduct when he believed he had acted rightly.

PAGE 114.

14. **On this ground:** Ministers do not often act without some kind
of a reason. On examination, Pitt's attitude, though somewhat inconsistent, is not so flagrant as it appears at first sight. It has already been
pointed out that there was at any rate a strong case to be made out on
behalf of the Rohilla war; that so far as it was a *political* error, based
on an erroneous idea of danger threatening from Rohilcund, it might
fairly be forgiven in view of subsequent services; and that the first
picture of the atrocities by which it had been accompanied was grossly
exaggerated. Besides, it had been in effect condoned by the re-appoint-
ment of Hastings as Governor-General. But in the Benares affair there
was certainly strong *prima facie* ground for suspecting that the demands
made by Hastings had been formulated with the direct intention of
driving the Rajah to resistance, and that it was consequently a case of
deliberate oppression. That Hastings was prepared to defend this
action did not make it the less a fair ground for impeachment. Pitt did
not accuse him of a mere error of judgment in the amount of the fine,

but of an oppressive intention. That is to say, Pitt's change of front was not so wholly devoid of plausibility as Macaulay implies, though he is probably correct in seeking for the real motive in political opportunism.

Page 115.

32. **works of supererogation**: superfluous deeds of virtue, which may count in the scale against sins. The doctrine is condemned in the Thirty-Nine Articles, on the ground that as perfection cannot be exceeded, and is itself the standard, superfluous virtue cannot exist.

Page 117.

8. **Board of Control**: the new board, constituted under the India Bill of 1784.

28. **prorogation**; the suspension of Parliament at the end of the session.

Page 118.

15. **Windham**, of whom Macaulay gives a description (p. 124), was a brilliant speaker, a man of great talents and high character, but an unmistakable failure.

Page 120.

3. **difficult to refute**: the House of Commons however hardly stood to the person impeached in the relation of a plaintiff in a private suit. The bias of the plaintiff is a recognised element in his evidence, but it would obviously be an advantage if such bias did *not* have to be allowed for; and known malice on his part would tell against his evidence. So, the Managers of the Impeachment would be in a worse position if they included a man who was known to bear private malice against the accused. It was hardly *unjust* to include Francis; but it would have been impolitic.

Page 121.

4. **Bacon**: Francis Bacon, Lord Verulam, was condemned in 1621 for corruption on the judicial bench as Lord Chancellor. It has however been maintained that the habit of receiving presents from suitors was practically universal and did not affect the judges' decisions.

5. **Somers**, a great Whig statesman, who took a prominent part in securing the accession of William III. He is a special favourite of Macaulay's. He was impeached and acquitted in 1701 for his share in the "Partition Treaties."

6. **Strafford**: the great minister of Charles I. Until his fall, he was held responsible for every unconstitutional act of the king's, though

many persons believe that not a few of those acts were perpetrated in the teeth of his advice. He was impeached in 1741, but conducted his defence with such ability that it became clear that the legal charge of treason would fall through. His opponents therefore proceeded by Bill of Attainder to which the king gave assent; and Strafford was beheaded.

19. **Eliott** had held Gibraltar though it was in a constant state of siege, from July 1779 till the repulse of the grand assault and the final relief in October 1782.

PAGE 122.

4. **Siddons**: Mrs Siddons, the great actress.
6. **the historian**: Gibbon, author of the *Decline and Fall of the Roman Empire*.
8. **Verres** was propraetor of the province of Sicily, where he was guilty of the grossest oppression. He was put on his trial, when Cicero's speeches against him were among that great orator's most eloquent efforts.
9. **Tacitus**, better known to fame as an austere, learned, and brilliant if by no means impartial historian, than as an orator. The reference here is to the trial of an African proconsul named Marius, under the emperor Nerva in A.D. 99; when Tacitus took a leading part in the prosecution.
12. **Reynolds**: Sir Joshua, first President of the Royal Academy.
15. **Parr**: Samuel Parr enjoyed in his own day an immense reputation for scholarship and erudition, but left no works of any value.
21. **her to whom**: Mrs Fitzherbert, to whom the Prince of Wales, afterwards George IV, was privately married.
23. **the Saint Cecilia**: Mrs Sheridan, whom Reynolds painted in the character of Saint Cecilia, the patron saint of musicians and reputed inventor of the organ.
25. **that brilliant society**, known as the "Blue-stocking society."
30. **Georgiana**, the celebrated Duchess of Devonshire, the most famous beauty of the day, whose portrait was painted by Gainsborough, was a very notable whig. When Charles James Fox stood for Westminster at the general election of 1784, the Duchess and her friends canvassed on his behalf with great zeal; a kiss from her was said to have been the price by which at least one stubborn political opponent was converted into a supporter.

PAGE 123.

14. **Mens aequa**, etc.: "a mind unmoved amid difficulties."
15. **proconsul** is a term used in effect to signify the governor of a

province of an Empire sufficiently distant from the central government to oblige him to take direct personal responsibility for the policy he pursues. In the days of the Roman Republic, the proconsul was one who exercised in a Province the powers held in Rome by a Consul. As a rule the office of proconsul was held the year after that of Consul: proconsuls being appointed to Provinces where there was war or danger of war. Under the the Empire, such officers were called "*legati Caesaris,*" the rulers of "peace" provinces being called proconsul, as under the Republic they had been called propraetor.

33. **bag**: i.e. bag-wig.

Page 124.

12. **Hyperides**, the contemporary and friend of Demosthenes.

22. **the youngest**: Charles Grey, afterwards Earl Grey, who became a great Whig leader, and head of the party which carried the great Reform Bill of 1832.

Page 125.

28. **Chancellor**: Lord Thurlow.

Page 126.

28. **Lord Loughborough**: Wedderburn, who had been Clive's great supporter.

Page 127.

10. **his father** had been an actor: but Sheridan himself as a writer of plays knew something of stage-effects.

30. **lacs**: a lac is a hundred thousand rupees: a **crore** is a hundred lacs; as computed in those days, about a million pounds: **zemindars**, landholders.

31. **aumils**, governors of a district: **sunnud**, a certificate of title: **perwannah**, a signed magistrate's order: **jaghire**, estate: **nuzzur**, a gift to a superior.

Page 128.

2. **Law**, afterwards Lord Ellenborough.

14. **the Regency**, see note supra, p. 110.

18. **the States-General**: the meeting of the States-General began the formal contest between the People and the Government of France which developed into the French Revolution.

27. **circuits**: the progress of the judges through the respective provincial districts, for conducting trials.

Page 131.

19. **the woolsack**: the seat on which the Lord Chancellor sits is so called.

24. **the great seal**: i.e. Lord Loughborough was now Lord Chancellor.

29. **junior barons**: i.e. the law-lords.

Page 132.

6. **violently and publicly**: Burke had openly in the House of Commons declared his friendship with Fox at an end, on May 6, 1791. Fox is said to have shed tears on the occasion.

Page 133.

14. **cuddy**: in the old merchant vessels, the equivalent of the saloon in the modern ship.

15. **Every gentleman**: it was particularly to be noted that Lord Cornwallis, who was the first Governor-General appointed under Pitt's India Bill, declared on his return to England that in India itself English and Native opinion were united in praise of Hastings.

Page 134.

82. **Logan**: a Scottish minister.

Page 135.

1. **Simpkin's letters**, written by a Captain Broome.

5. **Pasquin**; like the term *pasquinade* (=lampoon), the name was taken from a certain Pasquino, a tailor who lived in Rome in the 15th century and made a reputation for personal epigrams.

Page 136.

19. **a red riband**; part of the insignia of a knight of the Bath.

20. **at Whitehall**: i.e. a government appointment.

26. **Pitt retired** in 1801, in consequence of the king's refusal to concede Catholic emancipation to Ireland.

31. **Addington** became Prime Minister on Pitt's retirement.

32. **resigning the Treasury**: giving up the office of Prime Minister. Hastings no doubt looked at the question from a personal point of view. Addington had become an object of attack, therefore he ought not to surrender as long as he could hold his ground; nor was there any constitutional reason for his resignation as long as he could command a majority in the house. Addington however himself convinced Hastings that resignation was the right course.

22. Allipore: a suburb of Calcutta.

23. leechee: a fruit said to have been imported into India from China. Opinions differ: some Indians would like to see Mangoes in this country also.

31. Bootan, on the N.E. frontier of Bengal.

PAGE **138.**

7. Trissotin: a character in Molière's *Femmes Savantes*, bearing some resemblance to Sheridan's "Sir Benjamin Backbite" in the *School for Scandal.*

29. Dionysius, tyrant of Syracuse, 367—343 B.C., who was not only a patron of letters but liked to pose as a literary character himself.

Frederic the Great of Prussia, the most brilliant commander of his day, and one of the ablest monarchs of history, was more vain of his verses than of his statesmanship.

PAGE **139.**

1. Hayley, a younger contemporary and friend of Cowper. His verses enjoyed a brief popularity, but were essentially commonplace and perishable.

2. Seward: Anna Seward wrote elegiac and other poetry which received much applause from a few friends who knew no better. Her father also was what people called a poet before the revival of poetry a century ago.

PAGE **140.**

3. the Sheldonian Theatre: the building at Oxford in which degrees are conferred.

PAGE **141.**

19. a polity: i.e. a system of government. The whole administrative system of Bengal was constructed on the foundations Hastings had laid.

20. Richelieu: the great French minister when Charles I. was king of England and Louis XIII. of France.

21. Cosmo: the great Cosmo de Medici, who was supreme in Florence during the earlier half of the Fifteenth Century; an able and by no means scrupulous statesman, he obtained the title of "Father of his country," and was a very real patron of art and of letters.

INDEX.

*The reference given is to the page in the text of the essay in which,
or in a note on which, the subject is mentioned.*

Addington 136
Allahabad 27
American War 56
Asaph-ul-Dowlah 82-87
Augustulus 17
Aurungzebe 29, 57

Bacon 121
Begums 84-87, 117, 127
Benares 72
      Rajah of 73, 76-82, 114,
      127
Bengalee character 19
Bentinck, Lord W. 95
Black Hole 8
Bombay 39, 58
Bonaparte 137
Brahmins 46
Brooks's 105
Burke, Edmund 101, 103, 106,
   107, 111, 112, 119, 123, 128,
   130, 132, 134

Carnatic 8, 69
Champion 31, 32
Charles X. 74
Cheyte Sing 73, 76-87, 114, 127

Clarkson 107
Clavering 35, 46, 54, 55
Clive 7, 8, 9, 16
Coalition Ministry 103, 105
Commercial treaty 110
Constitutional rights 73-76
Coote, Sir Eyre 59, 71
Corah 27
Cossimbazar 8
Cowper, W. 6

Dallas 123
Daylesford 3, 135, 137
Devonshire, Duchess of 122
Dodd, Dr 109
Dundas 89, 112, 116, 117, 120,
   135
Dupleix 7
Dutch E. I. C. 8

Fitzherbert, Mrs 122
Forgery 20, 145
Fort William 8
Fox 105, 107, 113, 118, 123, 126,
   132
Francis, Philip 35, 41, 45, 61, 67,
   71, 106, 113, 119

French Revolution 110
      War 58
Fulda 9

Ghizni 28
Gibbon 122
Goldsmith, O. 1
Goordas 24, 42
Gordon, Lord G. 109
Grattan 101
Grenville, George 38
Grey, Lord 124, 132

Hafiz Rhamat 29
Hasting 3
Hastings, Howard 4
        Mrs 13, 55, 99, 101, 105, 135
        Pynaston 4
Holkar 57
Huntingdon, Earldom of 3
Hyder Ali 68-71

Imhoff 13, 105
Impeachment, the 121
        judgment in 132
Impey, Sir E. 6, 38, 44, 48, 65, 88, 90
India Bill, Fox's 105
        Pitt's 17, 117
Indiaman, life on 14
Ireland 56, 91

Jeffreys, Judge 66
Johnson, S. 13, 51
Jones, Sir W. 51, 95
Junius, letters of 35

Knox, Captain 33

Lally 59
Land-valuation 53
Lansdowne, Lord 90, 103
Las Casas 107

Law 123, 128
Law in India 62
Lely, Peter 3
Loughborough, Lord 102, 126, 131
Louis XI. 69

Machiavelli 2
Macleane, Col. 43, 52
Mahommed Reza Khan 18, 21-24, 41
Mahrattas 39, 57, 58, 68, 71
Mansfield, Lord 103
Marlborough, Duke of 93
Mayors of the Palace 17
Meer Jaffier 9, 21
Merovingians 17
Middlesex election 38
Mill, James 2
Monson 35, 53
Mysore 68

Nand Kumar, see Nuncomar
Nizam 69
North, Lord 34, 52, 56, 124
Nuncomar 19, 20, 22, 41-48, 77

Oates, Titus 49
Odoacer 17

Parr, Dr 122
Peers as judges 129
Pitt 112, 113, 117, 120, 124
Plassey 9, 59
Plomer 123
Popham 81
Porto Novo 71
Proconsuls 123

Ragoba 58
Regency Bill 110, 128
Regulating Act 34, 51
Reynolds, Sir J. 122
Rohilla War 29-33, 112
Rohilla character, 29, 33

St Lubin, Chevalier 58
Sandwich, Lord 52
Schitab Roy 23.24
Scindia 57
Scott, Major 31, 102, 110
Scott, Sir W. 1
Sevajee 57
Shah Alum 23, 27
Shelburne, 90. 103
Sheridan, R. B. 117, 127, 132
     Mrs 122, 126
Siddons, Mrs 122
Somers, Lord 121
Stafford, Lord 49
Stamp Act 109
Strafford, Lord 121
Subsidiary alliances 53
Sujah Dowlah 27, 29, 30. 32
Supreme Court 54, 61-65

Surajah Dowlah 8, 9
Sydney, Algernon 20

Teignmouth, Lord 100
Thurlow, Lord 113, 117, 125, 126,
   131
Tyler, Wat 63

Vansittart 10
Verres 122

Wedderburn 102, 126, 131
Wellington, Duke of 93
Westminster Hall 121
Wheler, 52, 71
Wilberforce 116
Wilkes 38
Windham 118, 124, 132

For EU product safety concerns, contact us at Calle de José Abascal, 56–1°, 28003 Madrid, Spain or eugpsr@cambridge.org.

www.ingramcontent.com/pod-product-compliance
Ingram Content Group UK Ltd.
Pitfield, Milton Keynes, MK11 3LW, UK
UKHW020317140625
459647UK00018B/1912